A Feast of Ice and Fire

A Feast of Ice and Fire

The Official Companion Cookbook

Chelsea Monroe-Cassel
and Sariann Lehrer

Bantam Books | New York

Published in the United States by Bantam Books,
an imprint of the Random House Publishing Group,
a division of Random House, Inc., New York.

BANTAM BOOKS and the rooster colophon are registered trademarks
of Random House, Inc.

Some of the recipes contained in this work were originally
published on the authors' blog, The Inn at the Crossroads,
www.innatthecrossroads.com.

Photographs on pages 2, 21, 35, 37, 66, 71, 78, 100, 139, 141,
145, 155, and 167 are by Kristin Teig and styled by Beth
Wickwire, copyright © Kristin Teig. Used courtesy of Kristin Teig.

All other photographs by Chelsea Monroe-Cassel and
Sariann Lehrer.

LIBRARY OF CONGRESS CATALOGING-IN-PUBLICATION DATA

Monroe-Cassel, Chelsea.
A feast of ice and fire : the official companion cookbook / Chelsea
Monroe-Cassel and Sariann Lehrer.
p. cm.
Includes bibliographical references and index.
ISBN 978-0-345-53449-1
ebook ISBN 978-0-345-53554-2
1. Cooking, International.   2. Cooking, Medieval.   3. Martin,
George R. R. Game of thrones.   I. Lehrer, Sariann.   II. Title.
TX725.A1M646 2012
641.59—dc23   2012009324

Printed in the United States of America

www.bantamdell.com

10 9 8 7

Book design by Virginia Norey

For Brent, for everything.

—CMC

And for all the cooks, chefs,
and powerful women who
inspired us along the way.

—SDL

Contents

Introduction

Come closer now. No, closer than that. I have a confession to make, an embarrassing confession, and I don't want everyone to hear. Another step, yes . . . lean close, and I'll whisper the sad truth in your ear:

I can't cook.

There 'tis, my shameful secret. All the paragraphs and pages that I've devoted to food in my books and stories over the years, all my loving and detailed descriptions of dishes both ordinary and exotic, all those fictional feasts that made your mouth water . . . I never actually cooked a single one of them. They were made of words. Big meaty nouns, crisp fresh verbs, a nice seasoning of adjectives and adverbs. Words. The stuff that dreams are made of . . . very tasty dreams, fat free and calorie free, but with no nutritive value.

Writing I'm good at. Cooking, not so much.

Well, okay, in the interest of full disclosure, I'm not bad at breakfast, so long as "breakfast" means frying up some thick-sliced bacon and scrambling a mess of eggs with onions, cheese, and just enough Italian seasoning. But when I want pancakes or eggs Benedict or (best) a breakfast burrito smothered in green chile, I head out to my favorite breakfast place (Tecolote Café in Santa Fe, New Mexico, for those who are keeping score). Like all red-blooded American males, come summertime, I have been known to stack up some charcoal briquets, douse them with lighter fluid, and char steaks, dogs, and burgers over the resultant blaze. Indoors, well . . . I can boil corn on the cob, I can steam veggies (when I must), and I do make a mean cheese-stuffed meat loaf. That's about the extent of it, though. That meat loaf represents the apex of my personal culinary achievement. When my wife broils a steak, it comes out charred on the outside and red on the inside. I broil the same steak in the same broiler, and it turns a uniform shade of pale gray throughout.

Fortunately, I am much better at eating food than cooking it (as a glance at my waistline will tell you, sad to say). Food is one of life's great pleasures, and I am all in favor of pleasure. Reading is another of those things that help make life worth living, and when one can combine reading and food, well . . .

Which is why my novels are so full of food—a trend that did not begin with A Song of Ice and Fire, I should note. A decade before I began writing *A Game of Thrones*, I recall, I attended the British version of the famous Milford Writers' Workshop and submitted a short story for critique. One of the other writers there called it "food porn." But then again, he was British, from the land of boiled beef and mushy peas. I have always suspected that the British Empire was largely a result of Englishmen spreading out across the world looking for something good to eat.

It *is* true that I spend a lot of words in my books describing the meals my characters are eating. More than most writers, I suspect. This does draw a certain amount of criticism from those readers and reviewers who like a brisker pace. "Do we really need all that detailed description of food?" these critics will ask. "What does it matter how many courses were served, whether the capons were nicely crisped, what sort of sauce the wild boar was cooked in?" Whether it is a seventy-seven-course wedding banquet or some outlaws sharing salt beef and apples around a campfire, these critics don't want to hear about it unless it advances the plot.

I bet they eat fast food while they're typing too.

I have a different outlook on these matters. I write to tell a story, and telling a story is not at all the same as advancing the plot. If the plot was all that mattered, none of us would need to read novels at all. The CliffsNotes would suffice. All you'll miss is . . . well, everything.

For me, the journey is what matters, not how quickly one can get to the final destination. When I read, as when I travel, I want to see the sights, smell the flowers, and, yes, taste the food. My goal as a writer has always been to create an immersive vicarious experience for my readers. When a reader puts down one of my novels, I want him to remember the events of the book as if he had *lived* them. And the way to do that is with sensory detail.

Sights, sounds, scents—those are the things that make a scene come alive. Battle, bedroom, or banquet table, it makes no matter; the same techniques apply. That's why I spend so much time and effort describing the food my characters eat: what it is, how it's prepared, what it looks like, what it smells like, what it tastes like. It grounds the scenes, gives them texture, makes them vivid and visceral and memorable. Sense impressions reach us on much deeper and more primal levels than intellectual discourse can ever hope to.

And the meals I describe do other things as well. World building is part of what gives epic fantasy its appeal, and food is part of that. You can learn a lot about a world and culture from what they eat (and what they won't eat). All you really need to know about hobbits can be learned from "nice crispy bacon" and "second breakfasts." And orcs . . . well, no one is likely to be doing *The Orc Cookbook* anytime soon.

The same is as true for individuals as for societies. There's a lot of characterization going on in those not-so-gratuitous feast scenes of mine. Oh, and sometimes that plot does advance as well.

Those are the side dishes, though. The main course here, the reason why I include such scenes in my fiction, is for the scenes themselves. I like writing about food, and my readers—most of them, anyway—seem to like reading about it. Judging by the number of readers who write to say that my feast scenes make their mouths water, I must be doing something right.

Unlike my world of Westeros or the real-life middle ages, the twenty-first century is a golden age, at least where food is concerned. Ours is an age of plenty, where foods of all types are readily available at any season, and even the most exotic spices can be purchased at the nearest grocery store, at prices that do not require you to mortgage your castle. Even better, for those of us who love to eat but cannot cook, this wonderful world of ours is full of people who will *cook for us.*

Enter Sariann and Chelsea.

At this late date, I can't possibly recall the first person to suggest we publish a cookbook with all the recipes from my novels. The first such suggestion probably came in not long after the publication of *A Game of Thrones* in 1996. Dozens of other readers have made the same suggestion in the decades since. Most of them were just tossing out the notion as a joke, to be sure—"You write so much about food, you ought to do a cookbook, ha ha." And even those who treated the idea seriously made the mistake of saying, "*You* ought to write a cookbook." Given my prowess in the kitchen, the chances of that happening were about equal to the chances of me writing an auto repair manual or a guide to computer programming.

Sariann and Chelsea were different. They did not just write to me and suggest that a cookbook would be a nifty idea, no. They actually began to cook some of the meals described in A Song of Ice and Fire, hunting up recipes in crumbling books of medieval cookery and pairing each with a more contemporary version made with modern, twenty-first-century techniques and ingredients.

They called their blog the Inn at the Crossroads, after a certain namesake establishment in the novels where various dire events take place. Among other things, the innkeep is hanged, and her corpse strung up outside the door to twist in the wind. A fate, I devoutly hope, that will not befall Sariann and Chelsea. Their food is much, much better than what is served at the original inn.

How do I know that? you may ask. Have I cooked any of these dishes, in either their medieval or modern versions? Well, no. I told you, I can't cook. I have *eaten* many of these dishes, however, and that's the important thing. When *A Dance with Dragons*, the most recent novel in the series, came out last July, I kicked off my book tour in Boston, and Sariann and Chelsea themselves showed up with a basket of lemon cakes, meat pies, and other goodies to keep me from feeling peckish during the signing. And thereafter, as I made my way from coast to coast, in a dozen different cities, confederates of theirs and readers of their blog turned up at most every signing, with more baskets and more dishes, each more toothsome than the last. And every basket featured lemon cakes. Sansa would have loved them.

Now that I am back home again, working on the next book, the baskets have stopped, alas. But fear not; we have this book instead, so you can cook your own versions of the favorite dishes of the Seven Kingdoms and the more exotic lands beyond. Those of you who cook can, anyway. And, hell, maybe even I will give a few of these recipes a try, assuming I can find a good source for dragon peppers. . . .

Eat hearty, my friends. Winter is coming.

George R. R. Martin
Santa Fe
January 21, 2012

About This Book

For many fans of the bestselling series A Song of Ice and Fire, reading these books is an immersive experience. Set in a quasi-medieval world, full of political intrigue, mayhem, and just a touch of magic, one defining quality of these books is George R. R. Martin's incredible attention to detail. He paints intimate portraits of his characters, embroidered with poignant descriptions of the landscapes they inhabit, the clothes they wear, and—our primary concern for this project—the foods they eat. It is a rare Martin reader who has never felt a pang of desire at the descriptions of dishes that are familiar enough to make the mouth water and exotic enough to stimulate the imagination.

Having often felt that stirring hunger as we read, we were eager to try our hands at turning fiction into an edible reality. It only took a few meals before we realized that we were really on to something. We launched our food blog, Inn at the Crossroads, shortly after and were delighted at how quickly it attracted an enthusiastic fan base. Just a few months after launching the blog, we were given the incredible opportunity to create this cookbook.

One needn't be a chef to enjoy the delicious fare of Westeros. Through our recipes, we aim to enable fans, regardless of how much or how little they know about cooking, to connect with their favorite fantasy series in a whole new way.

This cookbook is designed to take readers on a culinary journey through George R. R. Martin's world—beginning at the Wall, then gradually moving southward to King's Landing and Dorne, before taking ship across the narrow sea to feast with the Dothraki and in the Free Cities.

We can't tell you how much we've enjoyed our culinary adventures, but we can try to show you. So we hope that you will join us in your own kitchens for a feast unlike any you have prepared before: a feast of ice and fire.

Welcome to the Inn!
Chelsea & Sariann

A Feast of Ice and Fire

Stocking a Medieval Kitchen

While researching recipes for this cookbook, we found that our modern pantry was often insufficiently stocked with some of the quirkier ingredients called for in medieval, Roman, and Elizabethan cookbooks. Palates and preferences have changed through the centuries, usually with one taste replacing another. In this vein, we were able to satisfactorily replace the more scarce ingredients with those readily available in today's shops.

The key to successful cooking, whether in a medieval kitchen or a modern one, is innovation, so don't despair if you cannot find the exact meats or spices called for in a particular recipe. Rather, take a step back and look at the dish as a whole. Get a feel for the dish, based on where it is served, and go from there. To help you get started, we offer a few easy substitutions below.

Easier substitutions for meats:

Aurochs (a now extinct bovine species): beef or bison
Goat: lamb
Pigeon: duck or other dark meat poultry
Quail: game hens

Some wonderful and underappreciated herbs and spices, many of which can be found in specialty food stores or online:

Savory: Similar to thyme, but more subtle. May be directly substituted for thyme.
Grains of Paradise: Often included in mulled wine, this was a precursor to black pepper. Many medieval recipes call for grains of paradise, which, while peppery, has a more complex set of flavors than modern pepper. If unavailable, substitute slightly less black pepper.
Aleppo Pepper: Gives a wonderful rounded heat without a painful bite. Substitute paprika if unavailable.

Galangal: Related to ginger, this spice has a sweeter, subtler taste. The ground variety is the most versatile, and other forms should be ground likewise before using. Ground ginger is an acceptable substitute.

Sandalwood: A powdered form of red sandalwood was used primarily as a red dye in historical cooking. Sandalwood has a very mild spice flavor. Modern food coloring may be substituted.

Saffron: Imparts a yellow-orange hue to foods and a sweet, haylike scent and taste. Modern food coloring may be substituted for color.

Long Pepper: More unique and much stronger than black pepper, so it needs to be used carefully. If unavailable, simply substitute black pepper in equal portions.

Kitchen items that make period cooking easier:

A deep pie plate, preferably earthenware (Earthenware distributes heat evenly and steadily, unlike metal and glass.)

A proper pudding mold or basin (Absent from most American kitchens.)

A heavy, ovenproof saucepan

A chef's knife (One can never say enough about the wonders of a single sharp knife.)

The Basics

Poudre Douce

Poudre Forte

Medieval Black Pepper Sauce

Elizabethan Butter Sauce

Medieval Sauce for Fish

Roux

Medieval Pastry Dough

Medieval Sweet Dough

Lemon Pastry Dough

Poudre Douce

Poudre Douce, or "Sweet Powder," was a common medieval spice mix. Equally useful for flavoring savory main courses and sweet desserts, it was also used to season mulled wine, or hippocras. We've replaced the cassia flowers with extra cinnamon, although if ground cassia is available, two teaspoons may be used in place of half of the regular cinnamon.

> *Take four ounces of very fine cinnamon, two ounces of fine cassia flowers, an ounce of selected Mecca ginger, an ounce of grains of paradise, and a sixth [of an ounce] of nutmeg and galingale combined. Crush them all together. Take a good half ounce of this powder and eight ounces of sugar (which thus makes Sweet Powder) . . .* —LE VIANDIER DE TAILLEVENT, 14TH CENTURY

4½ teaspoons cinnamon

1 teaspoon ground ginger

1 teaspoon grains of paradise

Pinch of nutmeg

Pinch of galangal

1 cup sugar

Combine all the ingredients and store in a small airtight jar.

Poudre Forte

Poudre Forte, or "Strong Powder," was another of the commonly used spice mixes in the Middle Ages. The scents are reminiscent of holiday baking—clovey, but with a lovely bite to it.

Powder-fort . . . seems to be a mixture likewise of the warmer spices, pepper, ginger, &c. pulverized. —THE FORME OF CURY, 14TH CENTURY

1 teaspoon ground black pepper

1 teaspoon ground cinnamon

1 teaspoon ground mace

1 teaspoon ground ginger

1 teaspoon ground cloves

1 teaspoon long pepper or grains of paradise (optional)

Combine equal parts of all spices and store in a small airtight bottle.

Medieval Black Pepper Sauce

This recipe makes a rich sauce that pairs well with robust red meats, such as venison and boar, as well as the more mundane beef. The quantities of ingredients can be tweaked to make the sauce thicker or thinner to your preference, and you can adjust the amount of pepper to taste. The tartness of the vinegar might surprise you at first, but after a little acclimation, we think you'll like it as much as we do. The charred flavor of the bread combined with the bite of the pepper rounds out the flavor sensations that go with this sauce.

Poivre noir: Black Pepper Sauce. Grind ginger, round pepper and burnt toast, infuse this in vinegar and boil it. —LE VIANDIER DE TAILLEVENT, 14TH CENTURY

1 slice bread, toasted until black

⅓ cup verjuice, or equal parts cider vinegar and water

1 tablespoon red wine vinegar

1 tablespoon ground black pepper

¼ teaspoon ground ginger

Soak the burned bread in the liquid in a small saucepan until it falls apart, then mash it with a fork. Stir in the spices and slowly bring the sauce to a boil. For a thinner sauce, add more liquid; for a smoother version, press it through a sieve.

Elizabethan Butter Sauce

Makes about ¾ cup sauce

This recipe produces a quirky sauce, something like a rustic béarnaise. The butter lends it a decadent creaminess, while the lemon complicates the flavors in the best way. Ideal for serving with small poultry, such as quail.

> *A Sauce for a Roasted Pullet or Capon. When your Pullet is roasted and dished, put a little piece of Butter into the Belly at the end, with a little Claret, a hard yolk of an Egg minced, a Lemmon squeezed into it and Salt; give these one boyle with the Gravie and the Fowle in the dish, then garnish it with Lemmon and serve it up.*
> —THE ART OF COOKERY REFIN'D AND AUGMENTED, JOSEPH COOPER, 1654

1 hard-boiled egg yolk
½ cup white wine
4 tablespoons (½ stick) unsalted butter

1 tablespoon fresh lemon juice
Pinch of salt
Drippings (optional)

Mash the egg yolk with 1 teaspoon of the wine. Combine this with remaining wine, butter, and lemon juice in a small saucepan. Simmer, stirring constantly, for around 20 minutes to allow it to thicken a little. Drizzle over meat to serve.

Medieval Sauce for Fish

Makes about 2 cups sauce

This simple historical sauce pairs well with any fish. The combination of vinegar and ginger provides an interesting culinary experience, but it is subtle enough that it doesn't overpower the natural flavors of the fish.

> *Take Pykes and undo hem on þe wombes and waisshe hem clene and lay hem on a roost irne Þenne take gode wyne and powdour gynger & sugur, good wone, & salt, and boile it in an erthen panne & messe forth þe pyke & lay the sewe onoward.* —THE FORME OF CURY, 14TH CENTURY

2 cups red or white wine

1½ teaspoons ground ginger

2 tablespoons sugar or honey

Salt to taste

Prepare the sauce by bringing the wine to a boil. Reduce the heat, then add the remaining ingredients, stirring until the sugar is dissolved. Lay the grilled fish on a serving platter, then lightly cover with the sauce, or present the sauce as an accompaniment in a separate serving dish.

Roux

This is a wonderful trick to thicken your soups and stews. The flour works to thicken the broth, while the butter keeps the flour from becoming globby.

2 tablespoons unsalted butter

2 tablespoons flour

Melt the butter in a pan, stirring gently until it just starts to bubble. Add flour and mix completely with the butter. Stir until the mixture turns golden brown, just a few minutes. Add a ladleful of your soup broth to the pan, whisking constantly. Then pour this entire mix back into your soup pot, stirring thoroughly until the roux is all dissolved.

Medieval Pastry Dough

**Makes enough for eight 4-inch tarts, two 9-inch tarts,
or one 9-inch double-crust pie ✦ Prep: 10 minutes**

This recipe makes dough that is buttery and rich, and just perfect for both sweet and savory dishes.

> *Take fine floure and a curtesy of faire water and a disshe of swete butter and a litle saffron and the yolkes of two egges and make it thin and tender as ye maie.*
>
> —A PROPRE NEW BOOKE OF COKERY, 1545

Pinch of saffron	3 cups flour
½ cup water	2 egg yolks, slightly beaten
½ cup (1 stick) unsalted butter	

Dissolve the saffron in the water. Meanwhile, rub the butter into the flour with your fingers until there are only crumb-size pieces of butter left, then add the egg yolks and the saffron water. Stir until entirely incorporated, adding more water very gradually if needed, until everything just sticks together.

To prebake a shell, line a pan with dough, rolled very thin—to between ⅛ and ¼ inch. Using a fork, poke holes all over the bottom of the pastry shell, or use pie weights or dried beans to prevent bubbling. Bake for around 10 minutes at 350°F. Don't let the pastry start to brown! Remove it from the oven and fill as the recipe indicates.

Medieval Sweet Dough

Makes enough dough for fifty 2-inch pastries

This dough, when fried, creates a wonderfully old-fashioned-tasting cookie that is perfect for showcasing your favorite syrupy topping. Occasionally a bit hard, these are at their best when they're allowed to soak up the juices from the toppings.

. . . þan take fayre flowre, Safroun, Sugre, & Fayre Water, ande make þer-of
cakys, and let hem be þinne Inow . . .

—TWO FIFTEENTH-CENTURY COOKERY-BOOKS

4½ cups flour

2 cups sugar

Pinch of salt

2 teaspoons saffron (optional)

½ cup cold water, plus more if
needed

In a large bowl, mix together the flour, sugar, and salt. Dissolve the saffron by letting it sit in the cold water, then gradually work the water into the flour to make a smooth dough, similar to pie pastry. To achieve the right consistency, you may not use all the saffron water, or you may have to sprinkle in a little extra water.

Lemon Pastry Dough

Makes a single crust for a 9-inch pie ✦ Prep: 15 minutes

This recipe makes lovely dough that just begs to be made into fruit tarts. The lemon flavor comes through even after baking, sweet and tart.

1¼ cups flour, or more if needed

2 tablespoons confectioners' sugar

1 tablespoon cornstarch

Pinch of salt

7 tablespoons unsalted butter,
   softened to room temperature

Grated zest of 1 lemon

½ teaspoon vanilla extract

1 egg

Whisk the flour, sugar, cornstarch, and salt together, then cut in the butter until an even consistency resembling bread crumbs is formed. Add the zest, vanilla, and egg. Mix the dough with your hands until everything is incorporated. Add more flour, if needed, to create a dough that is not sticky. Flatten to a disk, wrap in plastic, and chill in the refrigerator for 30 minutes. Use as needed for the recipe.

Summary of Cuisine by Region

The Wall

The northernmost point in Westeros, the Wall is home to the Night's Watch: keepers of the 700-foot wall of ice, and the watchers in the night. It is a place that never gets warm and where the chill seeps into a person's bones. The Night's Watch is under-valued and underfunded, so they mostly eat whatever they can come by. Much of it is preserved—salt pork, salt cod, honeyed venison, and pickled foods. They also rely heavily on dried goods such as beans, peas, oats, nuts, and berries. Drinks of choice include hot wine and very heavy beer to help keep warm.

The North

A vast region nearly as large as the other kingdoms of Westeros combined, the North is ruled by the Starks in Winterfell. Their tables groan under the weight of roasted game, fowl, root vegetables, and baked goods. Apples, berries, squash, and a pleth-ora of seafoods feature heavily—though they occasionally receive goods from other parts of Westeros via the port in White Harbor. (Hence Sansa's affection for lemon cakes.)

The Vale

Much of the Vale of Arryn is made up of harsh, impassable mountains. However, in the Vale itself, the land is fertile and able to sustain the people who live around it. The Eyrie, the towering stronghold of House Arryn, serves up various sweets, including honeycomb and cakes, but also relies on meat from sturdy mountain animals like goats.

The Riverlands

Nestled in between forks of the river Trident, the fertile plains of the riverlands are ruled by House Tully. The rich soil allows for a wide variety of crops, while the rivers yield up plentiful trout, pike, and other fish. Leeks and other greens abound.

The Iron Islands

Like the members of the ruling House Greyjoy, the ironborn do not sow. The tables of these island people are laden with what can be harvested from the sea and what can be taken from others. Fish stews, crab stews, spiceless meats, and dark breads provide the basic nourishment for this region.

The Reach

The Reach is the southern breadbasket of Westeros. Here, rich agricultural lands yield the abundant bounty that has given Highgarden its reputation for prosperity. Dishes from this region are often prepared with the same courtly flair that distinguishes its ruling family, the Tyrells, who dine on delights such as cream swans, poached pears, and a wild array of fruit tarts.

Dorne

With a cuisine as fiery as the tempers of its people, the sandy region of Dorne features ingredients native to its desert reaches. Grilled snake and fire peppers are among the more unique ingredients, but the warm climate also produces copious olives, blood oranges, grapes, and dates.

King's Landing

As the largest harbor and city in Westeros, King's Landing is a melting pot, where all the peoples and cuisines of the realm come together. The highborn feast on swan, boar, partridge, and snails, while the commoners brave the infamous pot-shops for a bowl of dubious brown. Fruit is plentiful and features heavily in an assortment of cakes and tarts.

Across the Narrow Sea

The cuisine of the Free Cities and Dothraki sea is variable and exotic. Delectable treats like honeyfingers and fried locusts contrast with more rustic dishes such as dog sausage, crocodile, and spiny grubs.

The Wall

✦ ✦ ✦

Breakfast on the Wall ✦ *Applecakes*

Buns with Raisins, Pine Nuts, and Apple

Crusty White Bread ✦ *Salad at Castle Black*

Mutton in Onion-Ale Broth

Bean-and-Bacon Soup ✦ *Pork Pie*

Pease Porridge ✦ *Rack of Lamb*

Iced Blueberries in Sweet Cream

Mulled Wine

Breakfast on the Wall

When day broke, Jon walked to the kitchens as he did every dawn. Three-Finger Hobb said nothing as he gave him the Old Bear's breakfast. Today it was three brown eggs, boiled hard, with fried bread and ham steak and a bowl of wrinkled plums. —A GAME OF THRONES

Serves 1 + Cooking: 15 minutes

Pairs well with Black Bread (page 85),
Iced Blueberries in Sweet Cream (page 44), dark ale

This is a simple, hearty breakfast sure to give a good start to any day. The ham steak is more of a commitment than the other parts of the dish, but each element of the meal works well with the others. The eggs can be either fully hard-boiled, or left slightly soft so as to better pair with the fried bread, while the prunes add an appealing touch of sweetness that counters the salt of the ham.

1 breakfast ham steak	2 tablespoons unsalted butter
1 tablespoon oil	2 slices rustic bread
3 eggs	A handful of prunes

Sear the ham steak in a skillet with the oil until it starts browning, then set it aside on the serving plate and keep it warm.

To cook the eggs, place them in a small saucepan and cover with a finger's breadth of water. Bring the water to a simmer (not a boil), and simmer for 6 minutes. Cool the eggs rapidly by running them under cold water for 1 minute, and set them on the serving plate. For slightly softer eggs, cook for an initial 4½ minutes.

Melt the butter in the skillet you used for the ham and fry the slices of bread. Transfer the bread to the plate, add the prunes, and you're ready to break your fast!

Applecakes

*Jon was breaking his fast on applecakes and blood sausage when Samwell
Tarly plopped himself down on the bench. "I've been summoned to the
sept," Sam said in an excited whisper. "They're passing me out of train-
ing. I'm to be made a brother with the rest of you. Can you believe it?"*

—A GAME OF THRONES

Medieval Applecakes

Makes about 24

Prep: 20 minutes ✦ Dough rising: 1½ hours ✦ Frying: 30 minutes

Pairs well with Breakfast on the Wall (page 15), black pudding, cold milk

The clear predecessors of the modern doughnut, these medieval applecakes are soft,
chewy, and bursting with warm, nutty apple filling. Called *krapfen* in Germany, the
fluffy fried morsels are filled with nutty apple goodness.

*Einen krapfen. So du wilt einen vasten krapfen machen von nüzzen mit ganzem
kern. und nim als vil epfele dor under und snide sie würfeleht als der kern ist und
roest sie mit ein wenig honiges und mengez mit würtzen und tu ez uf die bleter
die do gemaht sin zu krapfen und loz ez backen und versaltz niht.*

—EIN BUCH VON GUTER SPISE, 1350

1¼ cups milk

2¼ teaspoons dry yeast (1 packet)

2 egg yolks, beaten

3 to 4 cups unsifted flour

Pinch of salt

4 tablespoons (½ stick) unsalted
  butter, softened

4 medium apples, peeled, cored,
  and diced

4 tablespoons honey

1 tablespoon Poudre Forte (see
  page 6)

1 tablespoon ground cinnamon

½ cup chopped nuts—walnuts, pecans, pine nuts, and chestnuts are all lovely

Oil for frying

Confectioners' sugar, for sprinkling (optional)

Warm the milk just slightly to the touch and then add the yeast to it. Let the mixture sit for 5 minutes until the yeast has foamed up. Add in the egg yolks, 3 cups of flour, the salt, and the butter. Mix thoroughly by hand until you have a soft dough that pulls away from the sides of the bowl, adding extra flour if needed.

Turn the dough out onto a floured countertop or board, and knead for several minutes, pushing with the heel of your hand, then gathering the dough back into a lump, adding more flour if necessary. Allow the dough to rise under a clean dishcloth for around an hour.

Meanwhile, in a medium saucepan, combine the apples, honey, spices, and nuts. Cook together over medium-low heat until the honey has been absorbed. Set aside and allow to cool slightly.

On the floured countertop, roll out the dough to ¼-inch thickness, dividing the dough in half if space is limited. Using a 2-inch round cutter, stamp out disks of dough, reserving the scraps to roll out again.

When you have made as many disks as possible, use a pastry brush or your fingers to wet each of them with water. On half of the dough disks, place about 1 teaspoon of the filling, then place another round on top. Press the edges together firmly to seal, and allow them to rise for around 20 minutes.

Heat 1 inch of oil in a pan over medium-high heat. Gently lower each cake into the hot oil with a slotted spoon. Fry until the dough is golden on both sides, about 4 minutes. Drain on paper towels, and sprinkle with a little confectioners' sugar, if you like.

Modern Applecakes

Makes 8 jumbo muffins ✦ Prep: 15 minutes ✦ Baking: 30 minutes

Pairs well with Breakfast on the Wall (page 15),
Honeyed Chicken (page 77), cold milk

Essentially apple coffeecake muffins, these have crumble tops with a crunch that contrasts with the softness of the cake itself. The apples melt as they bake, imbuing the cake with an incredible moistness and apple flavor.

For the Cake:

½ cup (1 stick) unsalted butter

1 cup granulated sugar

2 eggs

1 teaspoon vanilla extract

2 cups all-purpose flour

1 teaspoon baking powder

1 teaspoon baking soda

½ teaspoon salt

1 cup sour cream

2 to 3 tart apples, peeled, cored, and diced

For the Topping:

¾ cup packed brown sugar

1 teaspoon
ground cinnamon

2 tablespoons unsalted butter, chilled

½ cup chopped walnuts

Preheat the oven to 350°F. Grease the cups of a jumbo muffin pan.

In a large bowl, cream together the butter and sugar until light and fluffy. Beat in eggs and vanilla. In a separate bowl, combine the flour, baking powder, baking soda, and salt. Gradually add the dry mixture to the creamed mixture, alternating with sour cream and mixing well after each addition. Stir in the apples. Scrape the batter into the prepared muffin pan, filling each cup two-thirds full.

For the topping, combine the brown sugar and cinnamon. Cut in the butter until crumbly, then stir in the nuts. Sprinkle the topping evenly over the batter-filled cups, pressing gently to mix it with the cake. Bake for 30 minutes, or until a toothpick inserted near the center comes out clean. Allow to cool.

Buns with Raisins, Pine Nuts, and Apple

"Eat," Jon told him. "There's no knowing when you'll have another chance." He took two buns himself. The nuts were pine nuts, and besides the raisins there were bits of dried apple. —A STORM OF SWORDS

Elizabethan Buns with Raisins, Pine Nuts, and Dried Apple

Makes 12 buns + Prep: 45 minutes
Dough rising: 1 hour + Baking: 15 minutes

*Pairs well with Beef and Bacon Pie (page 71),
Salad at Castle Black (page 27), and Mulled Wine (page 48)*

These buns are made using a Banbury cake recipe. Banbury cakes are steeped in history and are thought to have been brought back to England during the Crusades. Their beautiful appearance belies their rugged durability; these buns are tasty high-energy food, sure to keep you warm while you range beyond the Wall.

Take a peck of pure Wheat-flower, six pound of Currans, halfe a pound of Sugar, two pound of Butter, halfe an ounce of Cloves and Mace, a pint and a halfe of

Ale-yeast, and a little Rose-water; then boyle as much new-milk as will serve to knead it, and when it is almost cold, put into it as much Sack as will thicken it, and so work it all together before a fire, pulling it two or three times in pieces, after make it up. —THE COMPLEAT COOK, 1671

For the Dough:

1 egg yolk	⅓ cup cream
⅓ cup dark ale, room temperature	1 teaspoon ground cinnamon
2 teaspoons yeast	1 teaspoon ground cloves
7 tablespoons unsalted butter	1 teaspoon ground mace
3¼ cups flour	Splash of rosewater (optional)
⅓ cup milk	

For the Filling:

3 cups currants	½ teaspoon ground mace
⅓ cup brown sugar	1 apple, chopped fine
½ teaspoon ground cinnamon	⅓ cup pine nuts
½ teaspoon ground cloves	

For the Glaze:

1 egg white, lightly beaten	⅓ cup raw sugar

To make the dough, whisk together the egg yolk, ale, and yeast, and place the bowl in a warm spot for 30 minutes.

Rub the butter into the flour until the mixture resembles bread crumbs. In a small saucepan, warm the milk and cream together with 1 teaspoon each of cinnamon, cloves, and mace. Pour the warmed milk, yeast mixture, and rosewater (if using) into the flour and mix together to form a dough. Knead the dough for 30 seconds, place it in a bowl, cover it with a tea towel, and let it rise for 1 hour.

To make the filling, take 5 ounces of the risen dough and put it in a food processor. Add 1 cup of the currants, the brown sugar, and the ½ teaspoon each of cinnamon, cloves, and mace. Pulse the mixture to combine it, pour it out into a bowl, and stir in the remaining currants, the apple, and the pine nuts.

Preheat the oven to 425°F and grease a large baking sheet. Cut the dough into quarters. Roll one piece into a long rectangle ⅛ inch thick. Cut the rectangle into three smaller rectangles. Spoon a heaping tablespoon of filling onto the middle of a rectangle and fold up the sides, pinching them together to seal. Once the bun is formed, gently fashion it into an oblong shape. Repeat with the remaining dough and filling, placing the completed buns on the greased baking sheet.

Brush the bun tops with the egg white and sprinkle them with the raw sugar. Slash the top of each bun three times and bake them for 15 minutes. These buns are wonderful served warm, but can also be cooled and stored in an airtight container for up to a week.

Modern Buns with Raisins, Pine Nuts, and Apple

Makes around 20 buns + Prep: 15 minutes
Dough Rising: 2½ hours total + Baking: 40 minutes

*Pairs well with Breakfast on the Wall (page 15),
Mutton in Onion-Ale Broth (page 29), cold milk*

These buns are a liberal interpretation of the baked goods described in the book. The brothers of the Night's Watch are probably not served gooey cinnamon rolls . . . but they are so delicious and bursting with tasty morsels that, after one bite, you'll forgive the liberties we've taken.

For the Dough:
¾ cup whole milk
4 tablespoons (½ stick) unsalted
    butter, softened
About 4 cups all-purpose flour

¼ cup sugar
2 eggs
2¼ teaspoons dry yeast (1 packet)
1 teaspoon salt

For the Filling:
1 apple, cored, peeled, and diced
⅓ cup raisins
¼ cup coarsely chopped pine nuts
1 cup brown sugar

2 tablespoons ground cinnamon
4 tablespoons (½ stick) unsalted
    butter, softened

For the Icing (optional):

1 cup confectioners' sugar   4 to 5 tablespoons milk

Combine the milk and butter in a small saucepan and scald the mixture, bringing it to just under a boil before transferring it to a large bowl and letting it cool to body temperature. Add 1 cup of the flour, the sugar, eggs, yeast, and salt. Add up to 3 additional cups of flour until the dough can be kneaded. Turn the dough out onto a lightly floured work surface. Knead the dough until it is smooth and elastic, adding more flour if it is sticky, for about 8 minutes. Form the dough into a ball.

Lightly oil a large bowl. Transfer the dough to the bowl, turning the ball to coat it with the oil. Cover the bowl with plastic wrap, then a kitchen towel, and let the dough rise in a warm, draft-free area until it is doubled in volume, about 1 hour.

Meanwhile, in a separate bowl, mix the apple, raisins, and nuts with the brown sugar and cinnamon.

When the dough has risen, punch it down. Transfer it to a floured work surface and roll it into a 22-by-11-inch rectangle. Spread the softened butter over the dough, leaving a ½-inch border. Sprinkle the apple mixture evenly over the butter. Starting on the long side, roll the dough into a log, pinching gently to keep it rolled up. With the seam side down and using a thin, sharp knife, cut the dough crosswise into slices about ¾ inch wide.

Grease a large baking sheet. Arrange the rolls on the sheet, almost touching one another. Cover the rolls loosely with a dishcloth and let rise for 40 to 45 minutes.

Position a rack in the center of the oven and preheat it to 350°F. Bake the rolls until the tops are golden, about 20 minutes, then invert them immediately onto a rack. Cool for 10 minutes. If making icing, mix confectioners' sugar with milk, adding one tablespoon of milk at a time, until a thick, pourable consistency is achieved. Drizzle over cooled rolls.

Crusty White Bread

The Great Hall of Winterfell was hazy with smoke and heavy with the smell of roasted meat and fresh-baked bread. —A GAME OF THRONES

Makes 3 small loaves ✦ Prep: 15 minutes
Dough rising: 3 hours to 2 days ✦ Baking: 30 minutes

Pairs well with Stewed Rabbit (page 94),
Rack of Lamb (page 42), butter and honey

This artisanal bread pairs well with just about any dish. The outside is crusty, the insides soft and moist. This is the ideal bread accompaniment to soups, stews, or even just a large pot of honey.

1½ tablespoons dry yeast (2 packets)	6½ cups all-purpose flour, plus more as needed
1 to 2 tablespoons honey	1 tablespoon coarse salt
3 cups warm water	⅓ cup cornmeal

Add the yeast and honey to the water and mix it up. Don't worry if all the yeast does not dissolve; it will finish mixing in the flour. Add the flour and salt and begin working them into the mixture.

Dump the dough onto a clean, floured countertop or board and knead for around 5 minutes, pushing with the heel of your hand, then gathering the dough back into a lump. Knead until the dough becomes one big mass. You will know when it is ready by poking it. When the dough bounces back, you're all set. If it's still too sticky, add a little extra flour.

Now place the dough into a large greased bowl, cover it with a towel, and let it sit in a warm place for about 2 hours. You can also put it in the refrigerator overnight; it will rise more slowly. You can even let the dough sit in the fridge for a couple of days, at which point it will begin to take on a slight sourdough taste.

Once the dough has at least doubled in size, divide it into thirds. Pull on each piece to form a ball, tucking all the ends in at the bottom. The balls should be semi-smooth. Dust the top of each round loaf with a bit of flour and make some light slices in the dough with a very sharp knife. Place the balls at least 4 inches apart on a baking sheet dusted with cornmeal and allow them to rise, uncovered, for about 40 minutes.

Preheat the oven to 450°F. Fill a baking dish or broiler pan with 2 cups of water and place it under the rack where your bread will go. (This is the trick to making a nice, crusty loaf of rustic bread. The steam from the water adds a nice crunch to the surface of the loaf.) Bake the loaves for around 30 minutes, until the crusts are a dark golden color and the loaves sound hollow when you tap them.

Salad at Castle Black

"From the Lord Commander's own table," Bowen Marsh told them. There were salads of spinach and chickpeas and turnip greens, and afterward bowls of iced blueberries and sweet cream. —A GAME OF THRONES

Serves 6 to 8 ✦ Prep: 10 minutes

Pairs well with Rack of Lamb (page 42),
Iced Blueberries in Sweet Cream (page 44), dark ale

The original recipe for salad comes from the 14th-century *Forme of Cury*. We took a few of the suggested greens and added turnip greens, raisins, and roasted chickpeas intended for snacking. We urge you to experiment with other combinations of greens as available, and we especially recommend adding sorrel and borage.

> *Salat. Take persel, sawge, grene garlec, chibolles, letys, leek, spinoches, borage, myntes, prymos, violettes, porrettes, fenel, and toun cressis, rosemarye, purslarye; laue and waishe hem clene. Pike hem. Pluk hem small wiþ þyn honde, and myng hem wel with rawe oile; lay on vyneger and salt, and serue it forth.*
>
> —THE FORME OF CURY, 14TH CENTURY

5 cups baby spinach

3 cups turnip greens

1 cup raisins

1 cup roasted chickpeas

Oil and vinegar to taste

Pinch of salt

In a large bowl, combine the greens, raisins, and chickpeas. Drizzle with oil and vinegar to taste, sprinkle with salt, and toss well.

✦ *Cook's Note:* The ingredients in the medieval recipe are parsley, sage, green garlic, scallions, lettuce, leek, spinach, borage, mints, primroses, violets, "porrettes" (green onions, scallions, and young leeks), fennel, garden cress, rosemary, and purslane.

Mutton in Onion-Ale Broth

The Wall wept and the sun crept across a hard blue sky. Near evenfall,
Owen the Oaf returned with a loaf of black bread and a pail of Hobb's
best mutton, cooked in a thick broth of ale and onions.

—A STORM OF SWORDS

Serves 3 to 4 ✦ Soaking wheat berries: 6 hours to overnight
Broth: 1 to 2 hours ✦ Prep: 10 minutes ✦ Cooking: 30 minutes

Pairs well with Black Bread (page 85),
Buttered Carrots (page 137), dark beer

This is an ideal meal to make with lamb leftovers, such as one might have after Easter, as it utilizes meaty bones, stale bread, and flat beer. We have added in or changed only a few things in the original 15th-century recipe. The onions go in whole and come out surprisingly sweet, and the flavors in the black bread suit the mutton dish very well. Overall, this is a primitive, hearty soup that is perfect for the brothers of the Night's Watch.

Oyle soppes. Take a good quantite of onyons, and myce hem, noyt to smale, &
seth hem in faire water, And take hem vppe; and then take a good quantite of
stale ale, as .iij. galons, And there-to take a pynte of goode oyle that is fraied,
and cast the oynons there-to, And lete al boyle togidre a grete [while]; and caste
there-to Saffron and salt, And þen put brede, in maner of brewes, and cast the
licour there-on, and serue hit forth hote.

—TWO FIFTEENTH-CENTURY COOKERY-BOOKS

About 1 pound lamb bones or
   bony stew meat
8 pearl onions, skinned
1 bottle dark beer, preferably flat

Pinch of saffron (optional)
½ cup wheat berries, soaked until
   soft (at least 6 hours or
   overnight)

Salt to taste

½ pound ground lamb, or reserved meat from bones

1 tablespoon unsalted butter or oil

Day-old bread slices, or toasted bread slices of your choice

If you are using stew meat, remove the meat from the bones and set it aside. Place the bones in a large pot, cover with water, and simmer for 1 to 2 hours. Skim the surface of the broth occasionally to remove scum and excess fat.

To the large pot of broth, add the onions, beer, saffron (if using), wheat berries, and salt. Bring the soup to a boil, then reduce the heat to a simmer and continue to cook for 15 to 30 minutes. While the broth is cooking, heat the butter in a skillet and gently brown the ground lamb or reserved stew meat. Add the meat to the broth pot and keep the stew warm until you are ready to serve.

Break the bread slices into large pieces and place them in the bottom of individual soup bowls, then ladle the hot soup over the bread. Serve immediately.

✦ *Cook's Note:* If you serve the bones with the broth, be sure to warn your diners, lest they be surprised by them. Personally, we love the way the bones look in the bowl, and like a brother of the Night's Watch, you can then be sure to get every scrap of meat!

Bean-and-Bacon Soup

[Sam] had not eaten since that bowl of bean-and-bacon soup with Pyp and Grenn. Well, except for the bread and cheese, but that was only a nibble, *he thought. That was when he took a quick glance at the empty platter, and spied the mouse feasting on the bread crumbs.*

—A FEAST FOR CROWS

Traditional Bean-and-Bacon Soup

Serves 4 to 6 + Prep: 20 minutes + Cooking: 1 hour

*Pairs well with Black Bread (page 85),
Sweetcorn Fritters (page 122), sharp cheese, ale*

This soup embodies the best kind of stick-to-your-ribs heartiness, ideal for the damp, bone-chilling sort of winter day that is the norm on the Wall. The vegetables all cook down until they are very tender, and each bite of soup contains a bit of everything. The fava beans are unusual enough that they defamiliarize what would otherwise be just a normal soup; it is easy to imagine this being served in the dim, chilly mess hall of Castle Black.

Soak in lukewarm water a quart of dry beans, lentils, or peas, drain and put them in a crockery kettle, with two leeks, half a head of celery, two middling sized onions, one carrot, two cloves, salt, and pepper, half a pound of bacon, or four ounces of butter; cover entirely with cold broth, set on the fire and boil gently till the whole is well cooked; then take from the fire, throw away the cloves, put the bacon aside, mash the beans and seasonings, strain them, and put back in the kettle with the broth in which they have been cooked; in case there should not be enough to cover the whole, add a little to it, set again on the fire, stir, give one boil, pour on croutons and serve.

—WHAT TO EAT, AND HOW TO COOK IT, 1863

2 leeks (white and light green parts
   only)

2 stalks celery

2 medium onions

1 carrot

Two 15-ounce cans fava beans
   (about 4 cups)

2 whole cloves

Salt and ground black pepper

6 cups beef broth

½ pound bacon (6 to 8 strips),
   cooked crispy and crumbled

To clean the leeks, cut the roots off just above the base. Cut off the tough, dark green top of the leek, and discard or save for making vegetable stock. Slice the stalk in half lengthwise, and rinse, fanning the leaves out to remove the dirt. Slice the leeks into thin crescents, and put into a bowl of water. Swirl the leeks in the water to remove any sediment. Remove the leeks and allow to drain on a towel.

Chop the celery, onions, and carrot into small chunks.

Combine all the ingredients except the bacon in a large pot. Add the broth and as much water as needed to cover everything. Simmer over medium heat for about 1 hour, keeping an eye on the level of the liquid, and adding water if needed.

When all the vegetables have gone soft, ladle out some of the extra broth and reserve it. Remove the cloves.

Mash the soup with a potato masher until there are no whole beans remaining. Don't be tempted to puree it with a modern device; this would ruin the rugged authenticity. If you want a thinner soup, add some of the reserved broth back in until you get the desired consistency.

Add the bacon, stir to incorporate, and serve.

Modern Bean-and-Bacon Soup

Serves 3 to 4 ✦ Prep: 10 minutes ✦ Cooking: 20 minutes

Pairs well with Crusty White Bread (page 25),
Pork Pie (page 35), Honey Biscuits (page 114), dry white wine

Wonderfully simple yet surprisingly elegant, this soup is rich in flavors without being too heavy. The beans give the soup body, while the feta melts into the puree, creating a near-perfect blend of tastes. The thyme adds a touch of sophistication, and the whole dish comes together beautifully.

3 strips of bacon, plus extra for garnish

1 teaspoon olive oil

1 small onion, diced

One 15-ounce can cannellini beans, rinsed and drained

1 teaspoon dried thyme, plus extra for garnish

2 cups chicken stock

¼ cup feta cheese, plus extra for garnish

¼ cup orzo

1 cup water

Salt and ground black pepper to taste

In a small skillet, cook the bacon over medium heat until it is well browned but not burned. Remove to a plate covered with paper towels to drain. Pour off all but 1 teaspoon of bacon fat from the pan. Add the olive oil to the remaining fat.

Add the diced onion to the skillet and sauté for 3 to 5 minutes, or until it is just starting to brown. Add the beans, thyme, and stock, then raise the heat to high. Bring the soup to a boil, then turn it down to a simmer. Half cover with a lid, and cook for 10 minutes.

Puree the soup either with an immersion blender, or in batches with an upright blender. Return the soup to medium heat, then add the feta, orzo, 2 strips of crumbled bacon, and water. Cook for 5 minutes, or until the pasta is tender. Season with salt and pepper.

Ladle the soup into individual bowls, crumble a bit of the leftover bacon on top, garnish with thyme and feta, and serve.

Pork Pie

"If I could fly, I'd be back at Castle Black eating a pork pie," said Sam.

—A CLASH OF KINGS

Medieval Pork Pie

Serves 6 to 8 + Prep: 15 minutes + Cooking: 45 minutes to 1 hour

Pairs well with Bean-and-Bacon Soup (page 31),
Cream Swans (page 111), dry cider

This medieval pork pie is nothing like the savory modern meat pies with which you may be familiar. This is a sweet meat pie, flavored with honey and ginger. If you enjoy pork served with sweet barbecue sauce, this is the dish for you.

To mak pyes of pairis tak and smyt fair buttes of pork and buttes of vele and put it to gedure in a pot with freshe brothe and put ther to a quantite of wyne and boile it tille it be enoughe then put it in to a treene vessele and put ther to raw yolks of eggs pouder of guinger sugur salt and mynced dates and raissins of corans and mak a good thyn paiste and mak coffyns and put it ther in and bak it welle and serue it. —A NOBLE BOKE OFF COOKRY, 16TH CENTURY*

1 ½ pounds ground pork
½ teaspoon salt
4 egg yolks
2 teaspoons ground ginger
¼ teaspoon ground black pepper
⅓ cup honey

½ cup dried currants
½ cup chopped dates
1 batch Medieval Pastry Dough
   (see page 9) or dough for a
   double-crust 9-inch pie,
   unbaked

Preheat the oven to 375°F.

Brown the pork in a skillet over medium heat. Let cool slightly, and mix well with the salt, egg yolks, spices, honey, and fruits. (The filling should be very moist.) Place the mixture in the pie shell and add the lid. Fold the top dough under the edge of the bottom crust and pinch the edges shut. Cut decorative steam holes in the top of the pastry, and bake for 45 minutes to 1 hour, or until golden brown.

✦ *Cook's Note:* This makes a great pairing with the Cream Swans, because you will be able to use the egg yolks for the pork pie, and the whites for the swans.

Modern Pork Pie

Serves 6 to 8 ✦ Prep: 15 minutes ✦ Cooking: 45 minutes to 1 hour

*Pairs well with White Beans and Bacon (page 149),
Baked Apples (page 80), sweet cider*

The modern pork pie is dense and savory. Drizzled with barbecue sauce, hot sauce, or ketchup, it is rendered utterly delicious. If, against all odds, you end up with left-overs, this pie is wonderful for a quick, cold breakfast straight from the fridge.

1 onion, diced

1½ pounds ground pork

1 sleeve of Ritz crackers, about 1½ to 2 cups crushed

1 tablespoon poultry seasoning

½ teaspoon ground cumin

Pinch each of salt and ground black pepper

⅓ cup spicy barbecue sauce, plus additional for serving

2 apples, cored, peeled, and thinly sliced

1 cup grated cheddar cheese

1 batch Medieval Pastry Dough (see page 9) or dough for a double-crust 9-inch pie, unbaked

Hot sauce and ketchup, for serving

Preheat the oven to 375°F.

Lightly brown the onion in a pan over medium heat. Place it, along with the pork, crackers, poultry seasoning, cumin, and salt and pepper, in a bowl and mix thoroughly. Pour the filling into the pie shell, spreading it out evenly. Brush the sauce over the pork mixture. Arrange a layer of sliced apples over the top of the sauce, then sprinkle the cheese over the top of the apples.

Cover with the second piece of dough. Fold the top dough under the edge of the bottom crust and pinch the edges shut. Cut decorative steam holes in the top of the pastry and bake for 45 minutes to 1 hour, or until golden brown. Serve with the option of BBQ sauce, hot sauce, or ketchup.

Pease Porridge

They ate oaten porridge in the mornings, pease porridge in the afternoons, and salt beef, salt cod, and salt mutton at night, and washed it down with ale. —A FEAST FOR CROWS

Medieval Pease Porridge

Serves 3 to 4 ✦ Cooking peas: 30 to 40 minutes ✦ Parboiling: 5 minutes

Pairs well with Crusty White Bread (page 25),
Pork Pie (page 35), dry or sweet cider

This medieval porridge is characterized by a surprisingly sophisticated undercurrent of herbs and spices. The pearl onions add flashes of flavor that provide sweetness, while the light color of the yellow peas helps highlight the green of the herbs and the orange of the saffron, making for an inviting-looking dish. It makes a nice first course for a summer dinner or a vibrant side accompaniment to a hearty main course.

French owt. Take and seeþ white peson and take oute þ perrey; & pboile erbis & hewe he grete, & cast he i a pot w the perrey pulle oynons & seeþ he hole wel i wat & do he to þ perrey w oile & salt; colo it with safron & messe it and cast þon powdo douce. —THE FORME OF CURY, 14TH CENTURY

2 cups dried yellow split peas
6 cups water
1 sprig fresh parsley
1 sprig fresh thyme
1 sprig fresh mint
12 pearl onions, peeled and
  left whole

½ teaspoon plus a pinch of
  saffron
2 tablespoons olive oil
Pinch of salt
1 teaspoon Poudre Douce
  (see page 5)

Put the split peas in a large pot, and add the water. Turn the heat up to medium high. Add the herbs and onions to the pot. Parboil the herbs for about 3 minutes, and the onions for 5 to 10 minutes, until they are soft. Using a slotted spoon, remove the herbs and onions from the pot and set the onions aside. Press the herbs dry and chop them finely. Cook the peas for about 30 to 40 minutes longer, or until they are soft. Drain the peas.

Place the cooked peas in a small saucepan and add the onions, chopped herbs, ½ teaspoon saffron, oil, and salt. Cook over medium heat for 5 minutes, stirring constantly to prevent sticking.

Place the pease porridge in a serving dish and sprinkle a pinch of saffron and poudre douce on top for color and flavor.

Modern Pease Porridge

Serves 4 ✦ Soaking peas: overnight
Prep: 5 minutes ✦ Cooking: 1½ to 2 hours

Pairs well with Trout Wrapped in Bacon (page 98),
Crusty White Bread (page 25), meat pies

If you like peas and onions, you will love this dish. This modern version is more sub-dued than the medieval recipe. It is best served warm and goes well with meats, cheeses, and other light lunch foods. Pease porridge is a traditional British side dish, and is still prepared today in one of two ways. The peas can be boiled in a pudding cloth, resulting in moister and softer porridge, or baked in the oven. The baked peas will be dryer, with delicious crispy bits on the top and around the edges.

8 ounces dried split peas
1 small onion, peeled
and halved

1 bunch fresh herbs, tied
together—consider thyme,
basil, and parsley

2 cups water

1 egg

Salt and ground black pepper
to taste

Beef stock or vegetable stock
(optional)

Pour peas in a bowl and cover them with at least a finger's breadth of water. Leave them to soak overnight at room temperature.

Drain the peas and put them in a pan with the onion, herbs, and water. Bring the mixture to a boil, then simmer, covered, until the peas are tender, about 1 hour. Stir occasionally, adding water if the mixture is drying out. Mash the peas by hand or in a food processor, then beat in the egg and season with salt and pepper.

From here, you can put the puree into the center of a floured pudding cloth, tie it securely, and boil it in stock for 1 hour, or spread it into a shallow, greased ovenproof dish, level the surface, and bake in the oven, preheated to 350°F, for 30 minutes.

✦ *Cook's Note:* A pudding cloth can be made out of any piece of cotton. Simply take a large square of cotton cloth and soak it in boiling water. Wring it out and lay it flat on your work surface. Take ½ cup of flour and spread it in a circle on the cloth. Dump the pudding into the center, pull up the sides, and tie well.

Rack of Lamb

The eight soon-to-be brothers feasted on rack of lamb baked in a crust of garlic and herbs, garnished with sprigs of mint, and surrounded by mashed yellow turnips swimming in butter. —A GAME OF THRONES

Serves 3 to 4 ✦ Prep: 20 minutes ✦ Cooking: 20 to 30 minutes

Pairs well with Buttered Carrots (page 137),
Modern Turnips in Butter (page 70), Arya's Snitched Tarts (page 100),
Southron Mulled Wine (page 48)

This is a fantastic dish for a dinner party. When cooked to perfection, the lamb will be pink and juicy on the inside and crispy brown on the outside. Each bite is tender and bursting with garlic and herb flavor.

2 racks of lamb, about 1¼ pounds each, frenched (about 12 chops)	1 cup soft fresh bread crumbs
	¼ cup olive oil
Salt and ground black pepper	1 tablespoon flour
2 cloves garlic, minced	¼ cup red wine vinegar
½ teaspoon dried parsley	Fresh mint for garnish (optional)
½ teaspoon dried thyme	

Position an oven rack in the middle of the oven and preheat it to 475°F.

Season the lamb with salt and pepper. Combine the garlic, parsley, thyme, and bread crumbs in a shallow bowl. Moisten the mixture with enough olive oil to hold it together, then set it aside.

Heat a large dry skillet over high heat. Put the rack of lamb, convex side down, in the skillet. With tongs, hold the meaty side against the skillet for a minute to give it a nice brown crust. Turn the rack to sear it on all sides for a total of 4 minutes. Remove the meat from the skillet and place it in a roasting pan, meat side up. Mix the flour and vinegar together in a small bowl, paint this mixture onto the lamb, then gently apply the herbed bread crumbs, patting them to form a crust covering the meat.

Roast the lamb until medium rare, 20 to 25 minutes (145°F internal temperature). For an extra-crispy crust, finish cooking the meat under the broiler for 2 minutes. Let the racks rest for 5 minutes.

To serve, use a carving knife to cut between the rib bones. Arrange the chops on warm serving plates. The chops are best served hot, and they will cool quickly, so you may want to carve them at the table.

Iced Blueberries in Sweet Cream

"From the Lord Commander's own table," Bowen Marsh told them. There were salads of spinach and chickpeas and turnip greens, and afterwards bowls of iced blueberries and sweet cream. —A GAME OF THRONES

Medieval Crème Bastard

Makes 4 large servings ✦ Freezing berries: 1 hour
Prep: 15 minutes ✦ Chilling cream: 2 to 3 hours

*Pairs well with Salad at Castle Black (page 27),
Rack of Lamb (page 42), Oatbread (page 125)*

This recipe produces an addictive cream sauce that is simple to make and not too sweet, complementing the natural sweetness of the berries. As a treat on the Wall, where Jon Snow makes his home, we thought it particularly fitting that the recipe is called Crème Bastard. Bastard is an early form of the word *custard,* and has no connection with one's parentage when used in a culinary context.

Take þe whyte of Eyroun a grete hepe, & putte it on a panne ful of Mylke, & let yt boyle; þen sesyn it so with Salt an hony a lytel; þen lat hit kele, & draw it þorw a straynoure, an take fayre Cowe mylke an draw yt with-all, & seson it with Sugre . . . —TWO FIFTEENTH-CENTURY COOKERY-BOOKS

1 pint fresh blueberries
2 egg whites, slightly beaten
1 cup plus 2 teaspoons milk
  or cream

2 tablespoons honey
Pinch of salt
2 teaspoons sugar

We prefer to start with fresh blueberries rather than frozen ones, because many frozen berries are often processed improperly. To get started, sort your blueberries,

setting aside any overripe ones for immediate snacking. The key is to freeze the berries flat, using a plate or baking sheet in the freezer. After the berries are frozen, they can be transferred to a bag and stored for up to six months.

While the berries are freezing, combine the egg whites and 1 cup of the milk in a pan on the stovetop, and bring to just under a boil, whisking all the while. Let it simmer for around 5 minutes, then add the honey and salt. After simmering for another minute or two, strain the mixture into a bowl. Add the remaining milk and sugar. Pour the sauce into a pitcher or serving dish and chill; it will thicken as it chills.

Pour the cooled sweet cream over the frozen berries to serve.

Modern Sweet Cream

Serves 4 + Freezing berries, chilling cream: 1 to 2 hours
Cooking cream: 20 minutes

Pairs well with Stewed Rabbit (page 94),
Roman Buttered Carrots (page 137), Honeyed Chicken (page 77)

This modern version of the dish is really just a sweeter, creamier version of the medieval preparation. It makes a refreshing dessert or a decadent breakfast. If the cream is allowed to thicken over the double boiler, custard is made.

1 pint fresh blueberries, frozen as for Medieval Crème Bastard (see page 44)	½ cup sugar
	5 egg yolks
	1 teaspoon vanilla extract
½ pint heavy whipping cream	Bowl of ice water

While the berries are freezing, combine the cream with half of the sugar in a medium saucepan and bring to a strong simmer—not a boil! Remove the saucepan from the heat.

Whisk the egg yolks and other half of the sugar in a bowl with a standing or hand mixer. Add the vanilla extract.

After mixing for 1 minute, begin *slowly* pouring the cream mixture down the side of the bowl, whisking rapidly to avoid curdling the eggs. After all the cream has been added, pour the mixture into a glass bowl that you can set atop a saucepan or into the top of a double boiler. Heat water in the bottom pan over medium heat and cook the sauce over it, stirring constantly, until it thickens to a pourable cream, about 10 minutes.

Set the glass bowl or top of the double boiler into the ice water to stop the cooking process. Stir the cream for 5 minutes to cool it, then pour it into a small pitcher and refrigerate.

Pour the cooled sweet cream over the frozen berries to serve.

Mulled Wine

The Old Bear was particular about his hot spiced wine. So much cinna-mon and so much nutmeg and so much honey, not a drop more. Raisins and nuts and dried berries, but no lemon, that was the rankest sort of southron heresy. . . . —A CLASH OF KINGS

Medieval Mulled Wine

Serves 4 + Prep: 5 minutes + Cooking: 20 minutes minimum

*Pairs well with Beef and Bacon Pie (page 77),
Aurochs Roasted with Leeks (page 75),
Medieval Honey Biscuits (page 114)*

This recipe produces a hearty mulled wine, rich in spices. It is heavy and strong, without the sweetness of many modern mulled wines. To accommodate the Old Bear's preferences, we added raisins, cranberries, and almonds to the 14th-century recipe, creating the ideal drink for those who plan to walk the Wall at night.

Hippocras. Take four ounces of very fine cinnamon, two ounces of fine cassia flowers, an ounce of selected Mecca ginger, an ounce of grains of paradise, and a sixth [of an ounce] of nutmeg and galingale combined. Crush them all together. Take a good half ounce of this powder and eight ounces of sugar [(which thus makes Sweet Powder)], and mix it with a quart of wine.
—LE VIANDIER DE TAILLEVENT, 14TH CENTURY

1 bottle inexpensive red wine
   (Cabernet Sauvignon, Malbec,
   and Pinot Noir are all
   good choices)

1½ tablespoons Poudre Douce
   (page 5)
Handful each of dried cranberries,
   raisins, and almonds

Bring the wine to a simmer. Stir in spice, nuts, and dried fruits, and continue to simmer for at least 20 minutes, stirring occasionally. After sitting, the spice mixture will create a thick residue that will settle to the bottom.

Using a ladle, serve into individual mugs or other heat-safe vessels. Try not to disturb the layer of spices at the bottom of the pot.

Southron Mulled Wine

Serves 10 ✦ Prep: 10 minutes ✦ Cooking: 45 minutes

Pairs well with Poached Pears (page 107),
Rack of Lamb (page 42), Arya's Snitched Tarts (page 100)

This recipe comes from the chaplain's wife at a top British university. It produces a delicious hot wine that, while spicy and rich, is medium-bodied and easy to drink. The sweetness of the honey and cane sugar combines brilliantly with spice of the fresh ginger, resulting in an arresting tingle that floods the palate without compromising the other flavors.

2 clementines or 1 small orange

20 whole cloves

2 bottles red wine (Shiraz and
Cabernet work well)

3 cups pulp-free orange juice

1 tablespoon ground cinnamon

2 cinnamon sticks

1 tablespoon ground nutmeg

Three 1-inch cubes fresh ginger

3 tablespoons honey

4 heaping tablespoons sugar

¼ cup fresh lemon juice

1 shot brandy, cognac, or Armagnac
(optional, but adds a pleasant
kick)

Slice the clementines in half and stud each half with the whole cloves, inserting the stem of the clove into the rind and leaving the buds protruding. You may need to pierce the flesh of the clementines with a small knife in order to insert the cloves. Float the clementines in the wine, rind down, so that the cloves are suspended in the wine.

Add all the remaining ingredients and bring the mixture to a simmer, stirring often with a whisk, but *do not boil*. Simmer for 5 minutes, then reduce the heat so that the wine is kept just below a simmer. Heat for 45 minutes, then serve with a ladle.

✦ *Cook's Note:* Don't be afraid to meddle with the proportions to suit your taste, adjusting the amounts of honey, ginger, and fruit juice as desired. Additional sugar or honey can also be added, to make the wine more drinkable for those who are not enduring freezing temperatures. The clementines make delicious boozy treats for the lucky guests still around when the wine runs out.

The North

✦ ✦ ✦

Breakfast at Winterfell

Oatcakes ✦ Cold Fruit Soup

Onions in Gravy ✦ Buttered Beets

Turnips in Butter ✦ Beef and Bacon Pie

Aurochs Roasted with Leeks

Honeyed Chicken ✦ Baked Apples

Breakfast at Winterfell

There was much more than [Catelyn] asked for: hot bread, butter and honey and blackberry preserves, a rasher of bacon and a soft-boiled egg, a wedge of cheese, a pot of mint tea. And with it came Maester Luwin.

—A GAME OF THRONES

Makes a big breakfast for 2 ✦ Prep: 5 minutes ✦ Eggs: 5 minutes

Pairs well with Crusty White Bread (page 25),
Applecakes (page 16), cold fresh milk

This meal presents an interesting textural array—the creaminess of the perfectly cooked soft-boiled egg, the crispiness of the bacon, and the pop of berry seeds all add something special. The continental elegance of the soft-boiled egg is a wonderful counterpart to the salty heartiness of the bacon. Likewise, the sweetness of the preserves and honey pairs well with the other elements. Go ahead and splurge on the bacon and eggs. If you truly wish your breakfast to have the feel of Winterfell, you shouldn't skimp on the ingredients. We recommend a nice cut of Black Forest bacon and free-range eggs. While the meal is fairly hefty, the mint tea lightens it more than one would expect and is the perfect finish to what might be the perfect breakfast. It's cold in the North, but this is a great breakfast for any time of year, anywhere.

2 eggs

6 strips bacon

4 small slices rustic bread

Butter, honey, and berry preserves

A sharp white cheese, such
  as cheddar

2 mint tea bags

Cook the bacon to your preference. Meanwhile, toast your bread, then butter it and add preserves, honey, or both. Heat water for tea. When the bacon is done, cover it with an overturned plate or a sheet of tin foil to keep it warm. Then you can focus on the eggs.

To cook the eggs, fill a saucepan about halfway with water and bring it to a simmer. Gently lower the eggs into the water one at a time. Cook the eggs for about 4 minutes. Don't wander off! (Although the worst that will happen is you'll have hard-boiled eggs, which are still yummy.) Using a slotted spoon, fish the eggs out of the hot water. Run them under cold tap water for 30 seconds to keep them from continuing to cook in the shell.

Pour hot water over the tea bags and steep them for a few minutes while you prepare the plates. Place the egg in an egg cup if you have one, or in the partially hollowed-out end of your bread loaf, as in the picture. Serve the eggs with the bacon, cheese, and toast alongside, accompanied by steaming cups of tea, and enjoy!

+ *Cook's Note:* To eat a soft-boiled egg, remove the top third of the eggshell. Use an egg cutter if you have one; otherwise, tap the shell with a knife or the edge of a spoon to crack it, forming a circle around the top. Carefully insert your knife or spoon into the egg and lever off the top. You'll know your egg is perfect if the white is reasonably firm and the yolk is hot but still runny. A small spoon, such as a teaspoon or grapefruit spoon, is the ideal utensil for scooping the egg out of its shell—there is even such a thing as an egg spoon.

Oatcakes

When they woke the next morning, the fire had gone out and the Liddle was gone, but he'd left a sausage for them, and a dozen oatcakes folded up neatly in a green and white cloth. Some of the cakes had pinenuts baked in them and some had blackberries. Bran ate one of each, and still did not know which sort he liked the best. —A STORM OF SWORDS

Traditional-style Oatcakes

Makes about 10 oatcakes ✦ Prep: 15 minutes ✦ Baking: 30 minutes

*Pairs well with Breakfast at Winterfell (page 53),
Leek Soup (page 87), butter and honey, tea or ale*

This recipe is loosely based on a traditional Scottish bannock, which at its core is a paste of oats and water cooked on a hot stone or griddle. We've assumed that the Liddle's oatcakes were baked at home in his kitchen, and we included ingredients accordingly. The resulting oatcakes are a unique combination of crisp and soft, dry and moist. Because of their texture, they are equally wonderful with tea or on a hike.

3½ cups old-fashioned rolled oats, not the quick-cooking variety

1 teaspoon salt

2 tablespoons flour

3 tablespoons honey, plus additional for serving

4 tablespoons (½ stick) unsalted butter, plus additional for serving

About ½ cup water

Handful of fresh berries of your choice (we used about 10 fresh blackberries)

Handful of pine nuts, roughly chopped

Jam for serving

Preheat the oven to 350°F. Lightly grease a baking sheet.

Combine the oats, salt, flour, and honey in a large bowl. Rub in the butter until the contents have a crumby texture. Add just enough of the water to dampen the dough so that you can roll it into a ball. Divide this mixture in two, pouring half into a second bowl. Add the berries to one bowl, and the pine nuts to the other, and mix thoroughly.

To form the cakes, pull off a piece of dough from one of your mixtures. Place a 3-inch-round cookie cutter on the greased baking sheet and press the dough into the cookie cutter. Alternately, you can form it into uneven rounds roughly the same size, sans cutter. In either case, your oatcakes should be no thicker than ¼ inch. Repeat with the other half of the dough.

Place the oatcakes on the baking sheet and bake for 30 minutes, or until lightly browned. (The berry version needs just a bit longer than the plain/pine nut version.) Transfer the oatcakes to a wire rack to cool. They are delicious plain, or with butter and honey or jam.

Modern Oatcakes

Makes about 14 sandwich cakes ✦ Prep: 15 minutes
Chilling: 1 hour ✦ Baking: 20 to 25 minutes
Assembly: 10 minutes

Pairs well with Breakfast in King's Landing (page 119),
Honeyed Chicken (page 77), hot tea

These crunchy oat cookies, neither too sweet nor too savory, sandwich jam and pine
nut fillings. They are great as dessert or a snack. Consider packing them with a lunch,
taking them on a picnic, or serving them as an accompaniment to tea.

½ cup (1 stick) unsalted butter,
    softened

¾ cup lightly packed dark brown
    sugar

1 large egg

1 teaspoon vanilla extract

½ teaspoon ground cinnamon

½ teaspoon ground ginger

Pinch of salt

¼ teaspoon baking powder

1 cup rolled oats

1½ cups flour, plus more for rolling
    and shaping dough

½ cup pine nuts

1 to 3 teaspoons olive oil

Blackberry jelly

Preheat oven to 350°F.

Mix together the butter and sugar until completely combined. Add the egg and vanilla, followed by the spices, stirring vigorously to mix everything. Add the remaining dry ingredients, making sure to fully incorporate each into the dough.

Divide the dough in half, then press each piece into a flat disk, wrap it in plastic, and chill in the refrigerator for 1 hour. Roll one disk out on a floured surface to a ¼-inch thickness. Using either a 3-inch-round cookie cutter or a similarly sized heart-shaped cookie cutter, cut out of the dough an even number of pieces. Arrange the cakes on a baking sheet and bake for 20 minutes, or until lightly golden. Remove cookies to a cooling rack. The finished oatcake sandwiches can be assembled while still warm, but not hot.

Meanwhile, finely chop the pine nuts in a food processor. Gradually add a small amount of olive oil at a time until the mixture takes on the consistency of a spreadable paste. Set aside.

When the oatcakes are baked, spread jam on ¼ of the cakes, then press another oatcake on top to form a sandwich. Repeat with the remaining oatcakes to make sandwiches with the pine nut puree.

Cold Fruit Soup

There were great joints of aurochs roasted with leeks, venison pies chunky with carrots, bacon, and mushrooms, mutton chops sauced in honey and cloves, savory duck, peppered boar, goose, skewers of pigeon and capon, beef-and-barley stew, cold fruit soup. —A CLASH OF KINGS

Medieval Cold Fruit Soup

Serves 2 ✦ Prep: 20 minutes ✦ Chilling: 1 to 2 hours

Pairs well with Breakfast at Winterfell (page 53), Modern Pork Pie (page 36), cold cider

On first spoonful, this soup comes across with just a strong honey taste. The color fools one's brain into expecting a different flavor—strawberry, perhaps—but once you're over the initial surprise, you can begin to appreciate it for its own merits. With a little cinnamon on top, the soup reminded us of a candied apple, yet the almond milk lends it just a bit of nuttiness.

> *Apple Muse.—Take Appelys an sethe hem, an Serge hem þorwe a Sefe in-to a potte; þanne take Almaunde Mylke & Hony, an caste þer-to, an gratid Brede, Safroun, Saunderys, & Salt a lytil, & caste all in þe potte & lete hem sethe; & loke þat þou stere it wyl, & serue it forth.*
>
> —TWO FIFTEENTH-CENTURY COOKERY-BOOKS.

2 firm, tart apples, peeled, cored, and sliced

1 cup almond milk

⅓ cup honey

1 tablespoon sandalwood powder (or enough red food coloring to tint the soup a light red)

Pinch of saffron

Pinch of salt

Poudre Douce (page 5) or cinnamon sugar for serving

Boil the apples until they become mushy, then drain them. Press the apples through a sieve, or whiz them in a food processor until they are mostly liquefied. Pour the apples into a saucepan and add the almond milk, honey, sandalwood, saffron, and salt. Cook, stirring, over medium heat until the soup thickens to a desirable consistency.

Place the soup in the refrigerator until it is chilled through, then serve it with poudre douce or cinnamon sugar on top.

Modern Cold Fruit Soup

Serves 8 ✦ Prep: 10 minutes ✦ Chilling: 1 to 2 hours, or overnight

*Pairs well with Breakfast in Meereen (page 193),
Oatcakes (page 55), fresh milk*

This is a simple, wholesome fruit soup. The melon and spices, combined with unusual herbs, results in a lovely yet unfamiliar combination of flavors, equally suited to the warmer seasons in the North and to the sweltering weather of exotic Meereen.

1 medium cantaloupe, cut into
   chunks
½ cup fat-free plain Greek yogurt
1 tablespoon grated fresh ginger
⅓ cup lemon basil leaves, or regular
   basil
Juice from 1 lemon

Pinch of sea salt
Pinch of ground cinnamon or
   ground nutmeg
Optional garnishes: a drizzle of
   honey, a few fresh basil or mint
   leaves, crushed nuts, a dollop of
   yogurt

Add the cantaloupe, yogurt, ginger, basil, lemon juice, salt, and cinnamon to a blender or food processor and blend until well combined. Refrigerate until completely chilled, preferably overnight. Dish into individual bowls, garnish as desired, and serve.

Onions in Gravy

Ben Stark laughed. "As I feared. Ah, well. I believe I was younger than you the first time I got truly and sincerely drunk." He snagged a roasted onion, dripping brown with gravy, from a nearby trencher and bit into it. It crunched. —A GAME OF THRONES

Serves 4 to 6 ✦ Prep: 5 minutes ✦ Cooking: 30 minutes

*Pairs well with Aurochs Roasted with Leeks (page 75),
Crusty White Bread (page 25), Baked Apples (page 80)*

Gravy, as we think of it today, evolved out of the ancient practice of using the drippings left from roasted meats to flavor other dishes; over time, it became a sauce in its own right. Here we have added whole onions to the gravy to make it more of a side than a sauce. However, as delicious as this recipe proves to be, it is at its best when paired with something. Bread, sharp cheeses, and roasted meat all suit admirably.

10 ounces boiler or pearl onions

1 tablespoon honey

1 tablespoon unsalted butter

1 sprig (about 1 teaspoon) of a
   finely chopped fresh savory
   herb, such as savory, rosemary,
   or thyme

⅓ cup apple cider

1 tablespoon flour

3 cups beef stock

Splash of brandy (optional)

Clean and peel the onions. Cut seven of the onions into quarters and set the remaining whole onions aside.

Place the honey into a deep frying pan over medium heat, along with the butter, herbs, and quartered onions. Stir to make sure the onions are covered with the butter and honey mixture, and cook for around 8 minutes, or until the onions begin to turn a nice golden brown. Stir all the while to make sure they don't burn.

Add the cider to the pan in three splashes, pausing for the liquid to heat between each splash. This will help deglaze the pan, dissolving all the lovely, sticky, tasty stuff into the gravy.

Sprinkle the flour over the pan and stir to make sure it fully incorporates into the gravy. Then add the stock and the reserved whole onions, and bring the mixture to a simmer. Continue to cook, stirring occasionally, for at least another 5 minutes, then reduce until it has reached the consistency you desire. At this point, check the taste; add the brandy if you're using it, season with salt and pepper according to your preference, and serve.

Buttered Beets

Then, for lack of any other books, [Tyrion] started reading them again.
The slave girl's story was the worst written but the most engrossing, and
that was the one he took down this evening to see him through a supper of
buttered beets, cold fish stew, and biscuits that could have been used to
drive nails. —A DANCE WITH DRAGONS

Traditional Buttered Beets

Serves 4 + Roasting: 45 to 60 minutes + Cooking: 10 minutes

Pairs well with Rack of Lamb (page 42),
Tyroshi Honeyfingers (page 202), red wine

This simple recipe showcases the best of beet flavor and texture, with the butter and vinegar subtly complementing the beets. Using different-colored beets adds a visual vibrancy to the dish, while still maintaining its rustic character.

When cooked, cut them in thin slices. Put butter in a stewpan, and when melted,
sprinkle in it a pinch of flour, a teaspoonful of chopped parsley, salt, and pepper,
then the beets; simmer twenty minutes, add a few drops of vinegar, and serve.
—WHAT TO EAT, AND HOW TO COOK IT, 1863

4 to 6 beets, preferably a mix of red
    and golden
Olive oil
4 tablespoons (½ stick) unsalted
    butter

1 teaspoon fresh parsley, finely
    chopped
Pinch each of salt and ground
    black pepper
Balsamic vinegar

Preheat the oven to 375°F.

Coat the beets lightly with oil and wrap them in aluminum foil; place them on a baking sheet and roast them in the oven until cooked through; this should take between 45 and 60 minutes.

Let the beets cool for 10 minutes, then peel and cut them into ¼-inch-thick slices.

Melt the butter in a saucepan, then add the parsley, salt, and pepper. Add the sliced beets, and stir to coat with the butter. Sauté for 5 to 10 minutes, sprinkle with a little balsamic vinegar, and serve.

✦ *Cook's Note:* Wrapping red and golden beets together in the same foil package produces a beautiful tie-dyed effect in the golden beets, giving them a remarkable sunset coloring.

Modern Beet Pancakes

Makes 4 pancakes ✦ Prep: 1 hour ✦ Cooking: 15 minutes

Pairs well with poached eggs, toast with jam, black tea

Beets make a fantastic alternative to traditional potato pancakes or hash browns. They turn sweet and tender when fried, and pair spectacularly with the creaminess of a poached egg.

2 whole beets, peeled and grated

1 shallot, chopped

Salt and ground black pepper

1 tablespoon olive oil

2 tablespoons unsalted butter

In a large bowl, mix the beets, shallot, and ¼ teaspoon each salt and pepper. Place the mixture in a colander and allow it to drain for 1 hour. Heat the oil and butter in a pan, then add the beet mixture in four pancakes. Flatten with a spatula to a thickness of about ½ inch, and allow the beets to cook for 5 minutes. Flip pancakes over and cook for an additional 3 minutes. Once browned on both sides, remove from heat, season with salt and pepper, and serve.

Turnips in Butter

The lord's seat at the head of the table had been left empty, but Robb sat to the right of it, with Bran across from him. They ate suckling pig that night, and pigeon pie, and turnips soaking in butter, and afterward the cook had promised honeycombs." —A GAME OF THRONES

Medieval Armored Turnips

Serves 3 to 4 ✦ Prep: 15 minutes ✦ Baking: 15 minutes

*Pairs well with Aurochs Roasted with Leeks (page 75),
Medieval Honey Biscuits (page 114), dark ale*

Turnips have sadly been pushed aside over time by their more modern cousin, the potato. However, this medieval recipe is rich and flavorful, and the turnips act as a delightful canvas for the cheese and spices. A historically accurate version of potato au gratin, the garnished turnips are lovely on any medieval table.

Rapam uel elixam uel sub cinere coctam in tessellas concides. Idem etiam facies de caseo subrecenti & pingui. Subtiliores tamen hae sint, quem quae ex rapis. In patellam butyro aut liquamine unctam. Primum tabulatum ex caseo facies secundum ex rapis, & sic deinceps, aromatum aliquid aut butyri continuo insundendo cito hoc pulmentum coquitur, cito etiam edendum est. —PLATINA, 1517

5 or 6 small turnips

1½ cups (6 ounces) mozzarella
or provolone

½ cup (4 ounces)
Parmesan

4 tablespoons (½ stick) unsalted
butter, melted, plus additional
soft butter for the dish

2 teaspoons Poudre Douce
(see page 5)

Preheat the oven to 350°F.

Peel the turnips, then boil them until tender, about 20 minutes, and allow them to cool. Meanwhile, grate or slice the mozzarella or provolone very thinly, and grate the Parmesan. Slice the cooled turnips about ⅛-inch thick.

Coat the bottom of a deep 9 x 9 inch or 9-inch-round baking dish with butter. Then arrange the ingredients in layers that are as thin as possible—first some cheese, then some turnips, then some butter, then some spice. Repeat the layers until ingredients are used up, keeping each layer as thin as possible. Top with more cheese. Bake until the cheese is just melted, around 15 minutes.

Modern Turnips in Butter

Serves 4 ✦ Prep: 10 minutes ✦ Cooking: 30 minutes

Pairs well with Modern Pork Pie (page 36),
White Beans and Bacon (page 149), Lemon Cakes (page 165)

These buttered turnips are nothing short of a miracle. The process of boiling the roots in milk creates a creamy, sweet, and tender result. Far and away the best turnip preparation we have ever tasted, this recipe will not disappoint!

3 large turnips, peeled and cut
    into similar-size pieces

3½ cups milk

3 sprigs fresh thyme

2 cloves garlic, peeled and chopped

½ cup (1 stick) unsalted butter, cut
    into cubes

Salt and ground black pepper to
    taste

Add the turnips, milk, and thyme to a large saucepan and simmer over medium heat for 20 minutes, or until the turnips are tender enough to stick a fork through with little resistance.

Drain the turnips, reserving the cooking liquid. Discard the thyme sprigs. Puree the turnips using a potato masher, immersion blender, or regular blender. Melt in the butter, add the chopped garlic, and continue blending. Add 2 cups of the reserved cooking liquid and combine until a uniform consistency is achieved. Season with salt and pepper and serve.

Beef and Bacon Pie

Part of him wanted nothing so much as to hear Bran laugh again, to sup on one of Gage's beef-and-bacon pies, to listen to Old Nan tell her tales of the children of the forest and Florian the Fool. —A GAME OF THRONES

Medieval Beef and Bacon Pie

Serves 6 to 8 ✦ Prep: 15 minutes ✦ Baking: 40 minutes

*Pairs well with Salad at Castle Black (page 27),
Roman Buttered Carrots (page 137), dark or hoppy beer*

We followed the recipe from *A Propre New Booke of Cokery*, simply swapping some thick-cut bacon in for the original marrow and letting the rest of the recipe be. The sweetness of the pie comes from the fruit, which dissolves as it cooks, providing a satisfying counterpoint to the tart vinegar and salty bacon. Then the fruit flavor fades into the background, and what remains is a sweet, rich meat pie with an easy medley of flavors.

> *To make Pyes. Pyes of mutton or beif must be fyne mynced & seasoned with pepper and salte and a lytel saffron to colour it, suet or marrow a good quantitie, a lytell vynegre, pruynes, great reasons, and dates, take the fattest of the broath of powdred beefe.* —A PROPRE NEW BOOKE OF COKERY, 1545

½ cup thick-cut bacon, diced or cut small

1½ pounds stew beef, cut into small pieces

½ teaspoon ground black pepper

½ teaspoon salt

¼ cup red wine vinegar

⅓ cup prunes, sliced

⅓ cup raisins

⅓ cup dates, chopped

1 cup beef broth

2 to 3 tablespoons flour

1 batch Medieval Pastry Dough (see page 9) or dough for a double-crust 9-inch pie, unbaked, rolled into 2 rounds

1 egg, beaten

Preheat the oven to 375°F.

Cook the diced bacon in a saucepan over medium heat until the fat runs from it, then drain off the fat. To the bacon pan, add the beef, spices, vinegar, and fruits. Add enough broth to thoroughly wet the mixture; the final consistency should be runny. Mix in the flour and cook on low heat until the juices form a gravy.

Let the meat mixture cool. Line a 9-inch pie pan with a round of pastry dough and fill it with the meat mixture. Add a pastry lid, turn the edges under, pinch them closed, and brush with beaten egg. Bake until the filling is bubbling and the pastry is cooked, about 40 minutes.

Modern Beef and Bacon Pie

Serves 8 ✦ Lattice: 15 minutes
Prep: 15 minutes ✦ Cooking: 1 to 1½ hours

Pairs well with Medieval Honey Biscuits (page 114),
Baked Apples (page 80), Mulled Wine (page 48)

This recipe is rich and savory, much closer to what we imagined when we read about the beef and bacon pies of Winterfell. For all that this is a relatively dense dish, the flavors are fairly light. The beef, bacon, onions, and herbs are all distinguishable, but don't linger overlong on the palate. The result is a lovely meat pie that can be served hot or cold.

12 strips bacon

2 tablespoons unsalted butter

1 onion, diced

1 carrot, cut into small chunks

½ medium potato, cubed

1½ pounds chuck steak or stew meat, cut small

2 tablespoons all-purpose flour

½ cup beef broth

Salt and ground black pepper to taste

Large pinch dried rosemary, or other savory herbs

½ batch Medieval Pastry Dough (see page 9), or enough dough for a single-crust 9-inch pie, unbaked

Preheat the oven to 400°F.

Weave the bacon strips into a lattice, alternating each strip under and over the others. Make your lattice as wide as you can, reserving any extra strips of bacon. Place this woven bacon and any extra strips on a baking sheet with high edges to catch the bacon grease. Bake for 15 to 20 minutes, or until the bacon is crispy. Set aside to cool, but leave the oven on to bake the pie.

Melt the butter in a pan over medium heat. Add the onion, carrot, and potato, and cook gently until the onion is soft and golden. Toss the beef with flour until each piece is covered. Add the beef to the vegetables and stir over low heat for 5 minutes, or until brown. Stir in any extra flour and cook for 1 minute longer.

Add the broth, salt, pepper, and rosemary; mix well, and simmer for 10 minutes, until a gravy has formed. Let the meat mixture cool.

Place your empty pie pan facedown on top of your lattice-work bacon. Using a sharp knife, cut around the pie pan until you have a circle of lattice. Crumble the leftover cooked bacon and add it to the filling.

Roll out the pastry dough and line your pie pan, allowing any extra dough to drape over the edge of the pan. Pour the filling mixture into the shell. Cover with the bacon lattice, pinching off any excess, then fold the extra dough over the top of the bacon. Bake for about 40 minutes, or until the crust is golden.

Aurochs Roasted with Leeks

Such food Bran had never seen; course after course after course, so much that he could not manage more than a bite or two of each dish. There were great joints of aurochs roasted with leeks, venison pies. . . .

—A CLASH OF KINGS

Serves 4 to 6 + Prep: 15 minutes

Sauce: 15 minutes + Cooking: 1 to 1½ hours

Pairs well with Baked Apples (page 80),
Onions in Gravy (page 62), Mulled Wine (page 48)

This is a very tasty main course, fit for any feast. The roasted vegetables are delicious—a counterpoint to the tender meat. They almost steal the thunder from the roast beef, but the addition of the black pepper sauce really kicks the meat up a few notches.

Top round of bison or beef,
  about 3 pounds
6 leeks (white and light green
  parts only), well washed and
  cut into ¼-inch slices
4 carrots, cut into ¼-inch slices
1 head of garlic, broken into
  individual cloves and peeled
Small bunch of fresh thyme,
  rosemary, bay, sage, or a mixture

Olive oil
Kosher salt and ground
  black pepper
Broth or water, if needed
  for basting
1 recipe Medieval Black Pepper
  Sauce (see page 6) for serving

Preheat the oven to 400°F and take the beef out of the fridge 30 minutes before it goes into the oven.

Place the vegetables, garlic, and herbs into a roasting tray and drizzle with olive oil. Toss to make sure everything is coated. Drizzle oil over the beef, then liberally sprinkle with salt and pepper. Place the meat directly on top of the vegetables.

Place the roasting tray in the preheated oven and cook for around 1 hour. Near the end of this time, check for doneness with a meat thermometer; 145°F should be about medium.

Check the vegetables halfway through the cooking process; if they look dry, baste them and the meat with juices from the tray. You can also add a splash of broth or water to keep them from scorching.

When the meat is cooked to your satisfaction, transfer it to a cutting board and allow it to rest for 15 minutes. Slice it thinly and serve it, drizzled with the sauce, with the vegetables alongside.

Honeyed Chicken

"Hungry again?" he asked. There was still half a honeyed chicken in the center of the table. Jon reached out to tear off a leg, then had a better idea. He knifed the bird whole and let the carcass slide to the floor between his legs. Ghost ripped into it in savage silence.

—A GAME OF THRONES

Serves 3 to 4 ✦ Prep: 15 minutes
Sauce: 30 minutes ✦ Cooking: 1 to 1½ hours

Pairs well with Crusty White Bread (page 25),
Modern Turnips in Butter (page 70), mead

This dish has a Northern feel. The apples, vinegar, honey, and dried berries invoke the chill of frosty evenings spent in the warm feast hall of Winterfell. The sauce reduces down to a thick, syrupy consistency, which melts enticingly when drizzled over the hot chicken. The dried fruits soak up the sauce and are bursting with flavor by the time they grace your plate.

1 whole chicken for roasting, about 6 pounds

2 tablespoons unsalted butter, melted

Salt

1 cup apple cider vinegar

⅔ cup honey

1 to 2 teaspoons mint, dried or fresh, chopped

½ cup currants, raisins, dried cherries, dried cranberries, etc.

1 tablespoon unsalted butter

Preheat the oven to 450°F.

Pat the chicken dry, then rub it down with melted butter and sprinkle with salt. This will make the skin crispy and delicious. Cook for approximately 1 hour, or until

the juices run clear when you pierce the thigh meat with a sharp knife and the breast meat is no longer pink.

While your chicken is roasting, combine all the remaining ingredients in a saucepan and allow the sauce to simmer until the dried fruit plumps and the sauce reduces to half its original volume, about 30 minutes. When the chicken is done, spread half the sauce and currants over the bird and reserve the other half to serve as gravy.

Baked Apples

[T]here were baked apples and berry tarts and pears poached in strong-wine. Wheels of white cheese were set at every table, above and below the salt, and flagons of hot spice wine and chilled autumn ale were passed up and down the tables. —A CLASH OF KINGS

17th-Century Baked Apples

Serves 2 to 4 ✦ Prep: 5 minutes ✦ Baking: 1 hour

Pairs well with Modern Pork Pie (page 36),
Aurochs Roasted with Leeks (page 75), white goat cheese, dry cider

This dessert is characterized by a rustic simplicity that evokes the sweetness and light of a 17th-century French countryside. Butter, sugar, and cinnamon, combined with the soft baked apple, make this something like an apple pie without the pastry crust.

Pommes au sucre. Pelez des pommes, fendez les en deux, ostez en le coeur, & le picquez par dessus. Emplissez en vostre plat a moitie, avec un peu d'eau, canella, beurre, & quantite de sucre. Faites les cuire a loisir avec un couvercle de four ou tourtiere. Estant cuites, seruez les sucrees.

—LE CUISINIER FRANCOIS, FRANCOIS PIERRE DE LA VARENNE, 1651

1 tablespoon ground
   cinnamon

4 tablespoons sugar

2 tablespoons unsalted butter,
   melted

2 firm, tart red apples

Preheat the oven to 350°F.

Mix together the cinnamon, sugar, and butter.

Slice the apples in half vertically through the core. Cut out the core and seeds (a melon baller or grapefruit spoon works well for this), then prick the inside of the apple all over with a sharp knife. Place the apples cut side up in a baking dish and pour in enough water to just cover the bottom of the dish. Divide the cinnamon filling among the apple halves, spreading it to coat the cut surface.

Cover and bake for 1 hour. Provide a fork and knife for your guests to eat the apples with, and enjoy!

Modern Baked Apples

Makes 8 baked apples ✦ Prep: 5 minutes ✦ Baking: 1 hour

Pairs well with Leek Soup (page 87),
Rack of Lamb (page 42), Mulled Wine (page 48)

These apples are a complex experience. The walnuts and dried fruit provide a textural counterpart to the smooth, maple-flavored sauce, while the spices add a lovely seasonality.

8 Granny Smith apples

¾ cup dried cherries or cranberries

¾ cup packed brown sugar

¼ cup coarsely chopped walnuts

2½ tablespoons pumpkin pie spice

1 cup apple juice

½ cup maple syrup

1 tablespoon unsalted butter

Preheat the oven to 350°F.

Hollow out the apples by cutting out the core from the top, leaving 1 inch of fruit on the bottom. Combine the cherries, brown sugar, walnuts, and spice and divide the filling among the apples, pressing it into the hollows. Place apples in a baking dish, cover them with tinfoil, and bake for 40 minutes. Uncover, baste with juices from the pan, and bake for another 25 minutes.

Meanwhile, heat the apple juice, maple syrup, and butter over medium heat until the mixture melts to form a smooth sauce.

Drizzle the apples with the sauce, and provide your guests with a fork and knife to eat with.

The South

✦ ✦ ✦

Black Bread ✦ *Leek Soup*

Sister's Stew

Broth of Seaweed and Clams

Stewed Rabbit ✦ *Trout Wrapped in Bacon*

Arya's Snitched Tarts ✦ *Blueberry Tarts*

Poached Pears ✦ *Cream Swans*

Honey Biscuits

Black Bread

The lower tables were crowded with knights, archers, and sellsword captains, tearing apart loaves of black bread to soak in their fish stew.

—A CLASH OF KINGS

Makes 2 loaves ✦ Prep: 15 minutes
Dough rising: 2 to 3 hours ✦ Baking: 25 to 30 minutes

*Pairs well with Sister's Stew (page 90),
Mutton in Onion-Ale Broth (page 29), dark beer*

This recipe is wildly easy, dense, and incredibly authentic-tasting. The flavor of the beer comes through in the finished loaf—a deep, earthy bitterness that is complemented by the small amount of honey. The inside of the loaf is soft, almost crumbly, while the crust bakes hard. It's ideal for creating a bread bowl for a bit of Sister's Stew.

Bread making and brewing have gone hand in hand practically since they both began, and it's only fitting that they should come together in this delicious bread. This recipe has no historical basis, as we created it from scratch, but it is so straightforward and the ingredients so simple that it could be made easily in Westeros.

2¼ teaspoons dry yeast (1 packet)
One 12-ounce bottle dark beer
   such as stout or porter, warm
2 tablespoons honey
2 teaspoons kosher salt
1 egg, beaten

4 to 5 cups mixed flour (we used 2
   cups white flour, 2 cups rye, and
   ½ cup whole wheat), plus
   additional white flour for
   working

In a small bowl, add the yeast and honey to the beer and allow the mixture to sit for 5 minutes until foamy. Add the salt and beaten egg to the wet ingredients, then begin adding in the mixed flour, one cup at a time. The ideal consistency for the dough is when it forms one cohesive mass. At this point, flour your work surface and turn the dough out for kneading. Using firm motions, knead the dough for about 5 minutes, until it bounces back when poked. Cover with a clean dish towel and let rise for at least 1 hour.

Punch down the dough, then replace the towel and let it rise again for at least 2 more hours, or refrigerate it overnight, which will give it just the slightest sourdough taste.

Preheat the oven to 450°F.

Form the dough into two loaves, dust them lightly with flour, and lightly slash the tops in a decorative pattern.

Bake for 25 to 30 minutes, or until the crust is nicely browned, then let it stand for at least 15 minutes before serving.

Leek Soup

The wedding feast began with a thin leek soup, followed by a salad of green beans, onions, and beets. . . . —A STORM OF SWORDS

Medieval Leek Soup

Serves 2 to 3 ✦ Prep: 10 minutes ✦ Cooking: 5 minutes

Pairs well with White Beans and Bacon (page 149),
Medieval Cheese-and-Onion Pie (page 143), dry white wine or cider

This recipe is quick to prepare, and the resulting broth has a bit of kick from the pepper and ginger. It's wonderfully fresh-tasting; paired with a chunk of sourdough bread, it's perfect for a spring evening's dinner.

Take funges and pare hem clere and dyce hem. Take leke and shrede hym small and do hym to seeþ in gode broth. Colour it with safron and do þer inne powdour fort. —FORME OF CURY, 14TH CENTURY

2 cups beef or chicken broth	1½ cups mushrooms, diced
6 threads saffron, or a pinch of ground saffron	¼ teaspoon ground ginger
	¼ teaspoon ground black pepper
1 leek (white and light green parts only), well washed and thinly sliced	¼ teaspoon salt
	Pinch of Poudre Forte (see page 6)

Place the broth in a medium saucepan. Add the saffron and bring the liquid to a boil. Add the leek, mushrooms, ginger, pepper, salt, and poudre forte to the broth, simmer for 3 to 4 minutes, then remove from the heat and serve.

Modern Leek Soup

Serves 4 ✦ Prep: 5 minutes ✦ Cooking: 45 minutes

*Pairs well with Crusty White Bread (page 25),
Almond Crusted Trout (page 156), Traditional-style Oatcakes (page 55)*

The addition of potatoes to this relatively modern recipe results in a creamy, rich texture that shows off the leeks to their best advantage. Thick and hearty, this soup is an ideal cold-weather comfort food.

4 tablespoons (½ stick) unsalted butter	2 large potatoes, peeled and chopped
2 leeks (white and light green parts only), well washed and chopped into thin rings	4 cups chicken broth
	Salt and ground black pepper to taste
1 small onion, peeled and finely chopped	Chopped fresh parsley for garnish

Heat 2 tablespoons of the butter in a large saucepan over medium heat. Add the chopped leeks and onion and cook, stirring, for about 5 minutes, or until the vegetables are soft but not brown.

Add the potatoes and cook for another 2 to 3 minutes, then add the chicken broth. Bring to a boil, then reduce the heat, cover, and allow to simmer for 35 minutes.

Using either a potato masher or an immersion blender, puree the soup until all the chunks of potato break down. Add the remaining butter. Season with salt and pepper, garnish with parsley, and serve.

Sister's Stew

The beer was brown, the bread black, the stew a creamy white. She served it in a trencher hollowed out of a stale loaf. It was thick with leeks, carrots, barley, and turnips white and yellow, along with clams and chunks of cod and crabmeat, swimming in a stock of heavy cream and butter. It was the sort of stew that warmed a man right down to his bones, just the thing for a wet, cold night. —A DANCE WITH DRAGONS

Serves 6 ✦ Soaking barley: 1 hour
Stock: 10 minutes ✦ Cooking: 45 minutes

*Pairs well with Black Bread (page 85),
Arya's Snitched Tarts (page 100), light beer such as a lager or pilsner*

This stew is exactly as good as it sounds in the book. The vegetables add a welcome splash of color that is absent from many seafood chowders. Despite the vast quantities of fish that go into the stew, it does not taste overly fishy. Instead, the seafood flavors melt into the creamy broth, mingling with the aromatic garlic and the subtle hint of saffron. Consider serving the stew in a hollowed loaf of black bread—this adds so many additional complex flavors that you will find yourself spooning up more and more to try to experience them all.

1½ pounds cod, cut into chunks

2 cups cold water

2 tablespoons unsalted butter

2 big leeks (white and light green parts only), well washed and chopped

2 large carrots, chopped

2 cloves garlic, minced

½ cup white wine

¼ teaspoon fresh thyme leaves

Salt and ground black pepper to taste

½ cup pearl barley, soaked for at least 1 hour in warm water

1 medium turnip, diced

1 cup heavy cream (do not try to go light and use half-and-half)

½ teaspoon crumbled saffron threads

One 12-ounce can evaporated milk

½ cup crabmeat, real or imitation

½ cup clam meat

Place ½ pound of the cod in a pot with the water. Bring to a boil and cook for 10 minutes. Then remove the fish with a slotted spoon and set it aside for later. Keep the water, as this is your fish stock.

In a large saucepan, melt the butter and sauté the leeks, carrots, and garlic over medium-low heat. Cook, stirring occasionally, until the vegetables are tender but not brown, about 5 minutes.

Add the wine and increase the heat, bringing it to a boil. Add the fish stock, thyme, salt, pepper, barley, and turnips; cook for about 20 minutes, or until the turnips are tender.

Warm the cream in a small saucepan—it should not even simmer—then rub the saffron threads into it until the cream turns a nice golden color. Stir the cream and evaporated milk into the broth and turnip mixture.

Add the remaining chunks of fish (both raw and cooked), the crab, and the clams. Cover and cook on medium low for 5 to 8 minutes, or until the fish is opaque. Serve hot.

Broth of Seaweed and Clams

When he woke the day was bright and windy. Aeron broke his fast on a broth of clams and seaweed cooked above a driftwood fire.

—A FEAST FOR CROWS

Serves 2 ✦ Soaking seaweed: 10 minutes
Clams: 5 minutes ✦ Cooking: 10 minutes

Pairs well with Black Bread (page 85),
Oatcakes (page 55), light beer such as a lager or pilsner

We can see why Damphair would love this intensely fishy and salty dish. Served piping hot with a warm chunk of bread for dipping, the broth has an unexpected depth. Butter and garlic, both traditionally paired with seafood, add extra flavor. As a breakfast, some may find it a bit strong on the palate, but seaweed is a great source of vitamins and minerals for those who want to start their day the ironborn way.

¼ cup dried wakame seaweed

8 fresh clams, rinsed and scrubbed

1 teaspoon unsalted butter

1 clove garlic, chopped

Ground black pepper to taste

Fill a large bowl with warm water and drop in the dried seaweed. Let it sit for 5 minutes, drain, and fill the bowl again. Let it stand for another 5 minutes, then drain out the water. Roughly chop the seaweed.

Place the clams, butter, and chopped garlic in a saucepan and add water until the clams are covered. Bring the water to a boil. Remove the clams as they pop open, reserving the broth in the pot. If any clams have not opened after you have been cooking them for 5 minutes, discard them.

While the clams are cooling, strain the cooking broth through a fine sieve and return it to the heat. Add the chopped seaweed and bring the broth to a boil.

To shuck the clams, pry open the shell halves and pull the meat out by hand.

Remove the broth from the heat, add the shucked clams, season with pepper, and serve.

+ *Cook's Note:* Seaweed can be found at grocery stores, in the Asian food section. We get ours from Whole Foods, where they have a variety to choose from. If wakame is not available, nori seaweed will work, and if seaweed isn't an option, kale can be used. Be sure to remove the tough and bitter central stem of the kale before cooking, and boil until tender before adding to your broth.

Stewed Rabbit

"You'll eat rabbit, or you won't eat. Roast rabbit on a spit would be quickest, if you've got a hunger. Or might be you'd like it stewed, with ale and onions."

Arya could almost taste the rabbit. "We have no coin, but we brought some carrots and cabbages we could trade you." —A STORM OF SWORDS

16th-Century Stewed Rabbit

Serves 4 ✦ Prep: 15 minutes ✦ Cooking: 2 hours 45 minutes

Pairs well with Black Bread (page 85),
Elizabethan Lemon Cakes (page 165), ale

Surprisingly tasty for a simple dish, this rabbit stew can be every bit as satisfying as much of Westeros' more sophisticated fare. Its rough simplicity lends the dish a level of authenticity. We swapped out the original wine for ale, but left the spices as they are in the period recipe, despite the fact that they probably would not be available at a country inn during times of hardship. The richness of the rabbit and the sour tinge of the vinegar make for a surprisingly dynamic flavor combination. By the end of the meal, you will be eagerly soaking up the remains of the broth with crusty bread.

[T]ake cony, henne, or malard and rost them till they be almost enoughe, or els chope them and fry them in freche grece and fry onyons mynced and put them in a pot and cast ther to freche brothe and half wyne clowes maces pouder of guinger and pepper and draw it with venygar and when it is boiled cast ther to thy licour and pouder of guingere and venygar and sesson it and serve it.

—A NOBLE BOKE OF COOKRY, 16TH CENTURY

4 tablespoons (½ stick) unsalted
 butter

1 medium onion, minced

1 rabbit, whole

2 slices bread, preferably stale

¼ teaspoon ground ginger

⅛ teaspoon mace

Pinch of cloves

Salt to taste

1 tablespoon red wine vinegar

½ cup carrots, finely chopped

½ cup cabbage, finely chopped

1 cup ale

Heat 2 tablespoons of the butter in a pan and fry the minced onion; transfer it to a pot large enough to accommodate the bones from the rabbit.

Cut the usable meat from the rabbit and lay it aside, leaving the legs whole. Break down the remaining bones and put them into a pot with the minced onion. Add enough water to cover, then bring the water to a boil, reduce it to a simmer, and cook until the meat starts to fall off the bone, about 2 hours. Strain out the bones and onion, and reserve the broth.

In a separate bowl, mix the bread with a few ladlefuls of broth. To this, add the spices, salt, and vinegar, then pour the mixture back in with the broth. Add the carrots and cabbage, and cook until the vegetables are soft, another 30 minutes or so.

In a medium pan, brown the rabbit legs and other meat pieces with the remaining butter. Deglaze the pan with the ale, then add both the meat and ale into the stewpot. Bring the stew to a boil, then serve.

Modern Stewed Rabbit

Serves 4 + Prep: 10 minutes + Cooking: 1 hour

Pairs well with Crusty White Bread (page 25),
Medieval Poached Pears (page 107), red wine

This dish is one of our favorites. While many of the soups and stews in Westeros rely on one or two simple, hearty flavors, this one is a distinct and sophisticated medley,

both rich and delicate at the same time. The rabbit takes on a sweetness from the wine and onions that blends divinely with the saltiness of the olives and is rounded out by the rosemary.

6 tablespoons extra-virgin olive oil

1 rabbit, cut into pieces, keeping the legs whole

Salt and ground black pepper

1 cup dry red wine

1 onion, finely chopped

1 carrot, chopped

2 stalks celery, chopped

2 tablespoons tomato paste

4 rosemary sprigs, tied into 2 bundles with kitchen string

3 cups chicken stock

½ pound Niçoise olives (1½ cups)

In a large, deep skillet, heat 2 tablespoons of the olive oil. Season the rabbit with salt and pepper. Brown the rabbit over medium-high heat, turning it occasionally, until it is crusty all over, about 10 minutes. Transfer the rabbit to a large plate.

Add the wine to the skillet and continue cooking, scraping up any browned bits on the bottom of the pan. Pour the wine into a cup and reserve, then wipe out the skillet.

Add the remaining ¼ cup olive oil to the skillet and reduce the heat to medium. Add the onion, carrot, and celery and cook, stirring occasionally, until softened, about 8 minutes. Add the tomato paste and rosemary bundles and cook, stirring, until the tomato paste begins to brown, about 5 minutes.

Add the rabbit and any accumulated juices along with the reserved wine to the skillet and cook, stirring occasionally, until sizzling, about 3 minutes. Add 2 cups of the stock, season with salt and pepper, and bring to a boil. Cover partially and cook over low heat for 30 minutes. Add the olives and the remaining 1 cup stock and cook until the sauce is slightly reduced and the rabbit is tender, about 20 minutes longer. Discard the rosemary bundles. Serve the rabbit in shallow bowls.

+ *Cook's Note:* Be mindful of the olive pits!

Trout Wrapped in Bacon

She stared at the supper set before her: trout wrapped in bacon, salad of turnip greens and red fennel and sweetgrass, pease and onions and hot bread. —A CLASH OF KINGS

Serves 2 + Prep: 10 minutes + Cooking: 10 minutes

Pairs well with Pease Porridge (page 38),
Turnips in Butter (page 68), Summer Greens Salad (page 133),
Medieval Fish Sauce (page 8)

The fattiness of the bacon melts just perfectly into the trout in this dish, and the rosemary adds a subtle flavor from the inside of the fish, while the Medieval Fish Sauce provides a tangy sweetness to the outside.

1 whole trout (10 to 12 ounces),   2 fresh rosemary sprigs
   cleaned and gutted   3 to 5 slices bacon
Salt and ground black pepper   3 lemon slices

Preheat the broiler.

Put the fish in a shallow baking pan or a large, heavy, ovenproof skillet, then pat it dry and season the cavity with salt and pepper. Put the rosemary inside the cavity and season the outside of the fish with salt and pepper, then wrap the bacon slices around the fish.

Broil the fish 5 to 7 inches from the heat until the fish skin and the bacon are crisp, about 5 minutes. Turn the fish over gently with a spatula and broil for 2 minutes longer. Add the lemon slices to the pan in a single layer alongside the fish and continue to broil until fish is just cooked through and the rest of the bacon is crisp, 2½ to 3 minutes longer.

Transfer the fish to a platter and serve.

Arya's Snitched Tarts

She filched one anyway, and ate it on her way out. It was stuffed with chopped nuts and fruit and cheese, the crust flaky and still warm from the oven. Eating Ser Amory's tart made Arya feel daring. Barefoot sure-foot lightfoot, she sang under her breath. I am the ghost in Harrenhal.

—A CLASH OF KINGS

Medieval Arya Tart

Prep: 15 minutes ✦ Frying pastry: 20 minutes
Topping: 45 minutes ✦ Yields: 50 tarts

*Pairs well with Honeyed Chicken (page 77),
Sansa Salad (page 135), Mulled Wine (page 48)*

These tarts take a while to make, but they are worth every minute. The pastries look like one could easily overindulge, but each small shortbread cookie is a commitment. The fruit syrup is heavy and chewy; our British readers may recognize this dessert as the medieval ancestor of the Jammie Dodger.

Take Wyn, & putte in a potte, an clarifyd hony, an Saunderys, pepir, Safroun,
Clowes, Maces, & Quybibys, & mynced Datys, Pynys and Roysonys of Corauns,
& a lytil Vynegre, & sethe it on þe fyre; an sethe fygys in Wyne, & grynde
hem, & draw hem þorw a straynoure, & caste þer-to, an lete hem boyle alle to-
gederys . . . þan kytte hem y lyke lechyngys, an caste hem in fayre Oyle, and fry
hem a lytil whyle; þanne take hem owt of þe panne, an caste in-to a vesselle with
þe Syrippe, & so serue hem forth, þe bryndonys an þe Sirippe, in a dysshe; & let
þe Sirippe be rennyng, & not to styf.

—TWO FIFTEENTH-CENTURY COOKERY-BOOKS

1 bottle inexpensive sweet red
  wine, such as a Shiraz
1½ cups honey
½ cup red wine vinegar
1 tablespoon Poudre Forte (see
  page 6)
½ cup chopped dates or prunes
½ cup currants

1 cup fresh or dried figs, if available
  (if not, substitute your favorite
  berries), diced
Crumbled candied nuts (optional,
  but delicious)
1 batch Medieval Sweet Dough
  (see page 9)
Vegetable oil for frying

Bring the wine and honey to a boil, then reduce the heat and skim off the foam until the liquid is clear. Add the vinegar, poudre forte, and fruits; return the mixture to a boil, then reduce the heat to a low simmer. Keep an eye on the fruit as you proceed—do not overreduce it! The syrup should lightly coat the back of a spoon and reduce by about a third to a half.

Roll the sweet dough to about ¼-inch thickness on a floured board, then use a circular cutter or drinking glass to cut out circles about 2 inches in diameter.

Pour a shallow layer of oil into a skillet or pan and place it over medium-high heat until hot. Working a few at a time, gently slip dough circles into the oil and fry until they are lightly browned and very crisp. Transfer the fried circles to paper towels to drain. Arrange the cakes on a serving platter, then spoon on just enough of the fruit mixture to cover each disk. Sprinkle with candied nuts. The yellowish cakes and the red topping make an interesting contrast in colors, and the wine will soften the cakes.

Modern Arya Tart

Makes 8 tarts + Prep: 15 minutes
Freezing: 30 minutes + Baking: 35 minutes

*Pairs well with Sister's Stew (page 90),
Honeyed Chicken (page 77), fruit wine*

These are simple confections that really impress. Flaky pastry, the classic combination of chèvre and apple, and the addition of honey and spices makes this a treat that is not to be missed.

Two 17.3-ounce packages frozen
    puff pastry (4 sheets), thawed
1 egg, beaten
6 ounces soft, fresh goat cheese
    (about ¾ cup packed)
1 tablespoon fresh lemon juice
¼ teaspoon kosher salt
3 medium Gala apples, peeled,
    quartered, cored, and cut into
    ⅛-inch-thick slices

3 tablespoons unsalted butter,
    melted
¼ cup honey, plus more
    for garnish
½ teaspoon ground allspice
½ cup chopped candied nuts
    (optional)

Line two rimmed baking sheets with parchment paper. Roll out each puff pastry sheet on a lightly floured surface to an 11-inch square. Using a 3- to 4-inch round cookie cutter or drinking glass, cut out four rounds from each pastry sheet to make sixteen total. Place four pastry rounds on each of the prepared baking sheets and pierce the dough all over with a fork.

Using a 3½-inch round cookie cutter or glass, cut out smaller rounds from the center of the remaining 8 rounds, forming rings. Brush the outer 1-inch edge of the solid rounds on the baking sheets with beaten egg, and top each with a pastry ring. Arrange the smaller rounds wherever they fit on the baking sheet. They make tasty snacks on their own with just honey and cinnamon. Freeze for at least 30 minutes.

Preheat the oven to 375°F.

Mix the cheese, lemon juice, and salt in a bowl, then spread the mixture inside the rings of the frozen pastry rounds. Overlap the apple slices on top.

Combine the butter and honey in a small bowl, then brush the mixture over the apples. Sprinkle the tarts with the allspice and nuts, if you're using them.

Bake until the apples are tender and the pastry is golden, about 35 minutes. Place the tartlets on plates. Drizzle a little honey over each and serve warm or at room temperature.

Blueberry Tarts

Sam loved to listen to music and make his own songs, to wear soft velvets, to play in the castle kitchen beside the cooks, drinking in the rich smells as he snitched lemon cakes and blueberry tarts. —A GAME OF THRONES

Medieval Blueberry Tarts

Makes 8 tarts ✦ Pie shell: 15 minutes
Prep: 15 minutes ✦ Baking: 45 minutes

*Pairs well with Trout Wrapped in Bacon (page 98),
Turnips in Butter (page 68), sweet wine*

These treats showcase the fresh fruits of summer. The custardy filling is rich without being overpowering, making it easy to eat several slices. The real focus of each tart is the fruit; the flavors of the berries come across beautifully.

Daryoles.—Take wine & Fr[e]ssche broth, Clowes, Maces, & Marow, & pouder of Gyngere, & Safroun, & let al boyle to-gederys, & put þer-to creme, (& yif it be clowtys, draw it þorwe a straynoure,) & yolkys of Eyroun, & melle hem to-gederys, & pore þe licoure þat þe Marow was soþyn yn þer-to; þan make fayre cofyns of fayre past, & put þe Marow þer-yn, & mynce datys, & strawberys in tyme of yere, & put þe cofyns in þe ovyn, & late hem harde a lytel; þan take hem owt, & put þe licoure þer-to, & late hem bake, & serue f[orth].

—TWO FIFTEENTH-CENTURY COOKERY-BOOKS

¼ cup milk

¾ cup heavy cream

¼ cup wine (a sweet red, such as
    Shiraz, is great)

Pinch of saffron

Pinch of ground ginger

Pinch of ground mace

Pinch of ground cloves

3 egg yolks

1 whole egg

½ cup honey

1 pint blueberries

½ cup chopped dates

1 batch Medieval Pastry Dough
  (see page 9), prebaked in eight
  4-inch tart pans and cooled

Preheat the oven to 375°F.

In a medium saucepan, combine the milk, cream, wine, saffron, and other spices. Bring the mixture to a boil, then remove it from the heat. In a separate bowl, beat the egg yolks, whole egg, and honey together. While beating, add ¼ cup of the hot milk mixture. Pour the egg mixture back into the pot with the hot liquid, whisking vigorously to avoid curdling.

Evenly spread the blueberries and dates into the cooled pie shells. Spoon the cream mixture over the fruit and into the shells. Bake for 45 minutes, or until the filling has set. Allow tarts to cool before slicing and serving.

Modern Blueberry Tarts

Makes one 9-inch tart to serve 6 to 8

Prep: 5 minutes ✦ Baking: 1 hour

Pairs well with Sansa Salad (page 135),
Medieval Leek Soup (page 87), champagne

These tarts are a favorite. They are delightfully fruity, but not overly sweet, relying on the natural flavor and sweetness of the berries to carry the dish. Served with a side of vanilla ice cream and a glass of champagne, this tart is the perfect summertime dessert.

1 batch Lemon Pastry Dough (see
  page 10)

2 tablespoons cinnamon sugar

2 pints blueberries

Confectioners' sugar for dusting

Preheat the oven to 375°F.

Press the dough into the bottom of a 9-inch round or square tart pan to an even thickness. Pour in as many berries as can fit in a single layer. Sprinkle the cinnamon sugar over the berries evenly, and pop the tart into the oven for 1 hour, or until the filling starts to bubble.

Remove the tart from the oven, top with any remaining blueberries, and dust with confectioners' sugar. Allow the tart to cool in the pan to room temperature before turning out and serving. Can also be served chilled.

Poached Pears

The war had not touched the fabled bounty of Highgarden. While singers
sang and tumblers tumbled, they began with pears poached in wine. . . .

—A CLASH OF KINGS

Medieval Poached Pears

Serves 2 to 4 ✦ Prep: 10 minutes
Cooking: 10 minutes ✦ Sauce: 20 minutes

Pairs well with Oatbread (page 125),
Modern Stewed Rabbit (page 96), red wine

Imbued with a vibrant pink color from the wine, these pears have a soft, warm texture and aren't overly sweet. The taste is reminiscent of mulled wine redolent with spices—an authentically medieval dessert, but every bit as delicious and satisfying as a modern dish.

Wardonys in syryp.—Take wardonys, an caste on a potte, and boyle hem till þey
ben tender; þan take hem vp and pare hem, and kytte hem in to pecys; take
y-now of powder of canel, a good quantyte, an caste it on red wyne, an draw it
þorw a straynour; caste sugre þer-to, an put it [in] an erþen pot, an let it boyle:
an þanne caste þe perys þer-to, an let boyle to-gederys, an whan þey have boyle
a whyle, take pouder of gyngere an caste þer-to, an a lytil venegre, an a lytil saf-
*ron . . . —*TWO FIFTEENTH-CENTURY COOKERY-BOOKS

2 to 4 firm, ripe, unblemished
   pears
1 teaspoon ground cinnamon
2 cups red wine
½ cup sugar or honey

¼ teaspoon ground ginger
1 tablespoon red wine vinegar
Pinch of saffron (optional)
Pinch of ground cloves (optional)

Parboil the pears in a large pot of water for about 5 minutes, then remove and peel. The pears look better presented whole, but can also be cut lengthwise, with their cores removed, if desired.

Heat the cinnamon, wine, and sugar in a pan over low heat until the mixture forms a smooth syrup.

Add the pears to the syrup and poach gently for about 10 minutes, keeping the syrup just below the simmering point to prevent the pears from falling apart. Near the end of the cooking period, add the ginger and vinegar, and, if you're using them, the saffron and cloves.

Let the pears cool in the syrup. If you have a lot of syrup left over, boil it down until it reduces somewhat, then pour it over the pears.

Modern Poached Pears

Serves 6 + Prep: 10 minutes
Cooking: 15 to 20 minutes + Sauce: 15 minutes

*Pairs well with Duck with Lemons (page 184),
Honey Biscuits (page 114), Tyroshi Pear Brandy (page 211),
vanilla ice cream*

This is an exquisite dessert. The caramel sauce is warm and gooey, with a subtle citrus flavor. It tastes of autumn—of crisp days spent in an orchard and evenings by the fire.

2 oranges

3 cups sugar

2 tablespoons honey

1⅔ cups water

6 large firm pears, peeled and
    cut flat on the base so that
    they stand upright

1 cup heavy cream

2 to 3 tablespoons Calvados

Vanilla ice cream or
    additional heavy cream
    for serving

Peel the oranges with a vegetable peeler; set aside the strips of zest, then juice the oranges.

Place the sugar in the center of a saucepan large enough to hold all the pears snugly. Add the honey and pour ⅔ cup of the water around the outside of the sugar. Heat slowly until the sugar has dissolved, gently stirring with a wooden spoon. Once the mixture starts to simmer, do not stir again. Watch for sugar crystals on the side of the pan and, if you see some, wash them down with a wet pastry brush. While you cook the syrup, heat the remaining 1 cup water until it boils.

Once the sugar mixture is a rich amber color (10 to 15 minutes), add the hot water, orange juice, orange peel, and pears. Do this *very* carefully, as the caramel will spatter. Cover the pot and simmer for 15 to 20 minutes until the pears are tender. Remove the pears and set them aside.

Remove the lid and add the cream and Calvados, then continue to simmer without out the lid until the caramel has reduced by about a third. Serve with vanilla ice cream or more cream drizzled on top.

+ *Cook's Note:* For an even more autumnal taste, try adding a pinch of cinnamon and ginger to the caramel along with the orange juice and pears.

Cream Swans

For the sweet, Lord Caswell's servants brought down trays of pastries from his castle kitchens, cream swans and spun-sugar unicorns, lemon cakes in the shape of roses, spiced honey biscuits and blackberry tarts, apple crisps and wheels of buttery cheese. —A CLASH OF KINGS

Makes 6 to 8 swans
Prep: 30 minutes + Baking: 1 hour 20 minutes

Pairs well with Trout Wrapped in Bacon (page 98),
Traditional Buttered Beets (page 65), any after-dinner liqueur

Absolutely delicious and beautiful in presentation, these swans involve a bit of preparation and assembly, but the oohs and aahs they produce from guests make the effort well worth it. The crispiness of the meringue combines with the frozen yogurt for a meltingly good partnership of texture and taste.

6 egg whites	Slivered almonds
½ teaspoon flour	High-quality vanilla ice cream,
1½ cups sugar (superfine is best)	frozen yogurt, gelato, or sorbet

Preheat the oven to 225°F.

Using a hand mixer, beat the egg whites and flour until soft peaks form. Gradually add in the sugar and beat on medium high until stiff peaks form (about 5 minutes—hang in there!). Load the mixture into a pastry bag (a large Ziploc with a corner snipped off works in a pinch). For beginning sculptors, select a basic round tip; the more adventurous can experiment with a variety of tips to get the look of feathers.

Place the template (see page 113) under a sheet of wax paper or parchment paper and pipe out the shapes for the base, wings, and neck with the head at one end. Place a slivered almond in each head for a beak. Keep in mind that meringue is fragile, and you will probably break a few elements, so make a few extra wings and necks.

Bake for about 40 minutes, then check on the necks, as they will finish first. Remove them if they are done, and continue to bake the rest of the pieces for about 40 minutes more. The finished meringue pieces should be light, dry, and crunchy. They can be stored in an airtight container at room temperature for several days.

To assemble the swans, lay out a base on a serving dish. Using a small ice cream scoop, make small balls of ice cream. Lay these on top of the base and attach the remaining elements of the swan. The wings go on the sides, and the neck on the front (use a chopstick or something similar to create a hole in the ice cream for the neck). Repeat to assemble all the remaining swans. Serve immediately.

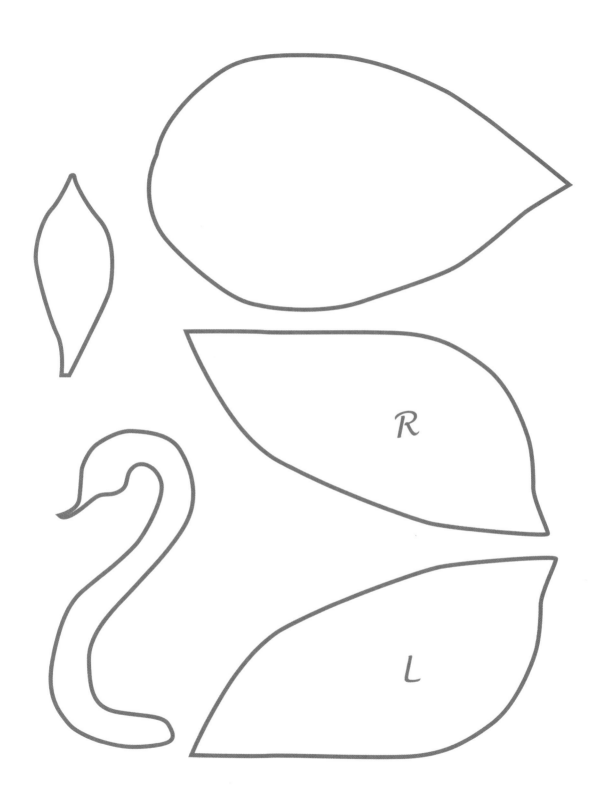

Honey Biscuits

For the sweet, Lord Caswell's servants brought down trays of pastries from his castle kitchens, cream swans and spun-sugar unicorns, lemon cakes in the shape of roses, spiced honey biscuits and blackberry tarts, apple crisps and wheels of buttery cheese. —A CLASH OF KINGS

Medieval Honey Biscuits

Makes about 20 biscuits ✦ Prep: 10 minutes ✦ Frying: 20 minutes

*Pairs well with any pie,
Bean-and-Bacon Soup (page 31), hot beverages*

These biscuits have a homey authenticity that comes from the use of plain pastry dough, dripping with honey and covered in cinnamon. They taste of warm cottages and comfort in a world where winter is coming.

> *Crispels. Take and make a foile of gode past as thynne as paper; kerue it out wyt a saucer & frye it in oile; oþer in grece; and þe remnaunt, take hony clarified and flamme þerwith. Alye hem vp and serue hem forth.*
>
> —CURYE ON INGLYSCH, 14TH CENTURY

2 cups flour	Olive oil or unsalted butter
1 teaspoon salt	¼ cup honey
5 tablespoons unsalted butter	1 tablespoon ground cinnamon
Cold water	

Mix together the flour and salt. Using your fingers, rub the butter into the flour until the dough has the texture of coarse bread crumbs. Gradually stir in just enough cold water that the dough sticks together. Be careful not to overwork it or add too much water.

Roll out the pastry to ¼-inch thickness and cut it into circles about 2 inches across.

Fry the pastry in a pan coated with a little olive oil or butter over medium heat, until lightly brown and crisp, being careful not to burn the pastry. This should take about 3 minutes. Drain well on paper towels. Meanwhile, place the honey in a saucepan and slowly bring it to a boil. Brush the pastries with the hot honey, sprinkle them with cinnamon, and serve hot.

+ *Cook's Note:* In place of a fresh batch of dough, feel free to utilize the leftovers from any of our pie recipes.

Modern Honey Biscuits

Makes 16 biscuits + Prep: 10 minutes + Baking: 15 minutes

Pairs well with Beef and Bacon Pie (page 71),
Sister's Stew (page 90), Iced Milk with Honey (page 169)

These biscuits are incredibly fragrant and bursting with spicy favor. They are served best warm with a tall glass of milk.

2 cups flour

1 tablespoon baking powder

1 teaspoon baking soda

1 teaspoon salt

1 tablespoon pumpkin pie spice or mixed spice	½ cup (1 stick) unsalted butter, chilled and cubed
½ cup granulated sugar	½ cup honey
2 teaspoons ground ginger	1 cup raw sugar for decorating

Preheat the oven to 300°F. Either line two baking sheets with parchment paper or plan to bake in two batches.

In a bowl, combine the flour, baking powder, baking soda, salt, spices, granulated sugar, and ginger. Using your fingers, rub the butter into the flour until the mixture resembles fine bread crumbs. Heat the honey in a small saucepan over medium heat until it is warm and runny (or microwave it for 1 minute). Add the honey to the flour mixture and work with a wooden spoon or spatula until a soft dough forms.

Pour the raw sugar into a bowl. Roll the dough into 2-inch balls and coat them with raw sugar. Place eight balls onto each prepared baking sheet, without flattening them; leave room around the sides for spreading. Bake for 12 to 15 minutes, or until the tops of the biscuits are just cracked. Let them stand on the baking sheets for 10 minutes before transferring them to a wire rack to cool.

Eat the biscuits right away or store them in an airtight container for up to a week.

King's Landing

✦ ✦ ✦

Breakfast in King's Landing ✦ *Fingerfish*

Sweetcorn Fritters ✦ *Oatbread*

Cream of Mushroom and Snail Soup

Sweet Pumpkin Soup ✦ *Summer Greens Salad*

Sansa Salad ✦ *Buttered Carrots*

Fish Tarts ✦ *Cheese-and-Onion Pie*

Pigeon Pie ✦ *White Beans and Bacon*

Bowls of Brown ✦ *Quails Drowned in Butter*

Almond Crusted Trout ✦ *Roasted Boar*

Peaches in Honey ✦ *Apricot Tarts*

Lemon Cakes ✦ *Iced Milk with Honey*

Breakfast in King's Landing

Cersei Lannister was breaking her fast when Sansa was ushered into her solar. "You may sit," the queen said graciously. "Are you hungry?" She gestured at the table. There was porridge, honey, milk, boiled eggs, and crisp fried fish. —A CLASH OF KINGS

Serves 2 + Porridge: 10 minutes to overnight
Fingerfish: 20 minutes + Eggs: 5 to 10 minutes

Pairs well with Oatbread (page 125),
Iced Milk with Honey (page 169), fresh fruit

This makes for a satisfying start to any day. The saltiness of the fingerfish is a flavorful counterpart to the sweetness of the honeyed porridge. The texturally aware eater will delight in the wide array provided by this spread: crunchy fish, soft porridge, thick honey, firm egg. Alternatively, present the selection as a smorgasbord so that guests can pick and choose.

1 recipe Traditional Fingerfish
   (see page 120), cooked and kept
   warm
1½ cups steel cut oats, soaked in
   water overnight
Milk (whatever you most
   commonly use is fine)

4 hard- or soft-boiled eggs
   (see page 15 or 54)
Berries, brown sugar, diced apples,
   nuts, honey, and other
   porridge toppings

Drain the soaked oats and pour them into a pot, adding just enough milk to cover them. Place the lid on the pot and cook over medium-low heat for 10 minutes. Meanwhile, prepare the eggs to your liking.

Arrange all the breakfast elements on your plate, and enjoy!

Fingerfish

In the Queen's Ballroom they broke their fast on honeycakes baked with blackberries and nuts, gammon steaks, bacon, fingerfish crisped in bread-crumbs, autumn pears, and a Dornish dish of onions, cheese, and chopped eggs cooked up with fiery peppers. —A STORM OF SWORDS

Traditional Fingerfish

Makes 10 fingerfish + Prep: 10 minutes + Frying: 15 minutes

Pairs well with breakfasts,
Traditional Bean-and-Bacon Soup (page 31),
Crusty White Bread (page 25)

The traditional recipe is one made on the Turkish coast of the Black Sea, where these fantastic little fish are a staple food. The outside is crunchy from the cornmeal bread-ing, while the inside is tender and moist. Just a pinch of salt brings out the taste of the fish, while a bit of lemon is a classic pairing.

10 hamsi (European anchovies), or other very small fresh fish such as sardines or smelt	Oil for frying
	Pinch of salt
	½ lemon (optional)
1 cup cornmeal	

You may either fry the little fish whole or take their heads off first. When they are sufficiently small, such as hamsi, they do not require deboning, but can be eaten whole.

Rinse the fish under cold water, then dip them in the cornmeal, coating them thoroughly.

Heat the oil in a skillet over medium-high heat. Fry the fish until they are lightly golden on both sides. Sprinkle with salt and squeeze a few drops of lemon juice over the fish, if desired, before serving.

Modern Fingerfish

Serves 2 + Prep: 15 minutes + Frying: 10 minutes

Pairs well with Pease Porridge (page 38),
Modern Bean-and-Bacon Soup (page 33), Lemonsweet (page 187)

This is a fish stick in perfect form. Miles beyond anything that came out of your mom's freezer when growing up, the batter is crispy, the fish tender and flaky. Add a squeeze of lemon and some tartar sauce, and you'll feel like a kid again.

1 pound halibut	3 tablespoons olive oil
⅓ cup flour	Lemon wedges for serving (optional)
1 large egg, lightly beaten	
1 cup panko bread crumbs	Tartar sauce for serving (optional)
2 tablespoons unsalted butter	

Cut the halibut into roughly fish-stick-shaped rectangles, and pat the pieces dry with a paper towel. Set out three shallow bowls and fill them with the flour, egg, and bread crumbs, respectively. Roll the fish pieces in the flour, then the egg, then the bread crumbs, covering every surface, and set them aside.

Melt the butter and olive oil in a pan over medium-high heat. Add the fish to the pan, and brown it on every side. Drain the fish pieces on paper towels. Serve with lemon wedges and tartar sauce on the side, if you like.

Sweetcorn Fritters

Tyrion listened with half a ear, as he sampled sweetcorn fritters and hot oatbread baked with bits of date, apple, and orange, and gnawed on the rib of a wild boar. —A STORM OF SWORDS

Serves 2 to 3 + Prep: 5 minutes + Cooking: 5 to 10 minutes

Pairs well with Oatbread (page 125),
Roasted Boar (page 157), light beer, such as a lager or pilsner

These are so very delicious. The batter crisps up during the frying, but the kernels of corn maintain their fantastic fresh pop. The result is a textural tug-of-war that will have you grabbing fritter after fritter. Given the lack of corn in Medieval Europe,

there are no extant recipes for corn fritters from that time period. As such, we have created a recipe that produces corn fritters that are flavorful, aesthetically consistent with Martin's description, and would pair well with the other foods he mentions in the passage.

2 tablespoons unsalted butter

Pinch of salt

Kernels from 2 ears cooked corn,
 or 2 cups frozen or drained,
 canned corn

1 large egg

¼ cup milk

⅓ cup yellow cornmeal

⅓ cup all-purpose flour

Pinch of ground black pepper

2 to 3 tablespoons vegetable oil

Melt the butter in a nonstick skillet over medium heat and sauté the corn kernels for about 5 minutes; sprinkle the corn with salt and set aside. In a separate bowl, whisk together the egg and milk until smooth, then stir in the cornmeal, flour, a pinch of pepper, followed by the corn.

Heat 2 tablespoons of oil in the same nonstick skillet over medium heat until hot but not smoking, then drop in 2 tablespoons of batter at a time. Fry until the fritters are golden brown on each side, around 5 minutes total, then transfer them to paper towels to drain. Cook all the batter in this way, adding more oil if necessary. Serve hot.

Oatbread

Tyrion listened with half a ear as he sampled sweetcorn fritters and hot oatbread baked with bits of date, apple, and orange, and gnawed on the ribs of a wild boar. —A STORM OF SWORDS

Makes 2 loaves ✦ Prep: 5 minutes
Dough rising: 2 hours total ✦ Baking: 30 minutes

Pairs well with any roasted fowl, Sweetcorn Fritters (page 123),
Iced Milk with Honey (page 169), butter and honey

Each bite of this bread has a different combination of fruity filling, but the entire loaf is soft and delicious, with the oats providing a subtle heartiness. A bite with a bit of candied orange peel is so utterly sweet and wonderful that it will keep you coming back for more and more.

1½ cups warm water	1 tablespoon kosher salt
2¼ teaspoons dry yeast (1 packet)	2 tablespoons unsalted butter,
2 tablespoons honey	at room temperature
1½ cups rolled oats	⅓ cup diced dates
2½ to 3 cups all-purpose flour	⅓ cup diced candied orange peel
(feel free to use some oat flour	⅓ cup peeled, diced apple
here, too), plus more as needed	Rolled oats for topping (optional)

In a large mixing bowl, combine the warm water, yeast, and honey. Allow the mixture to sit for around 5 minutes, until it becomes bubbly.

Add the oats, 1 cup of the flour, the salt, and butter to the yeasted water. Stir until completely mixed together, then add the fruits and work the mixture until they are evenly distributed throughout. Gradually add the rest of the flour until you have a cohesive mass of dough.

Flour a board or your countertop, and turn the dough out onto it. Adding flour as needed, knead the dough for around 8 minutes. If you poke it and it bounces back, you're done.

Place the dough in a greased bowl and cover it with a clean dish towel. Put it in a warm place until it has doubled in size. Then punch it down and divide it in half. Form the dough into two round loaves. Wet the top of each loaf with a little water, then sprinkle it with rolled oats. Using a sharp knife, lightly score the top with an X shape.

Place these loaves on a baking sheet and allow them to sit, covered with a clean tea towel, for about 1 hour, or until they have doubled in size again.

Preheat the oven to 400°F.

Bake the loaves for around 30 minutes, or until they are golden brown.

Ideally, you should allow the loaves to cool for at least 10 minutes before cutting into one, but given how good this bread smells, you might have trouble leaving it alone.

Cream of Mushroom and Snail Soup

The first dish was a creamy soup of mushrooms and buttered snails, served in gilded bowls. Tyrion had scarcely touched the breakfast, and the wine had already gone to his head, so the food was welcome. He finished quickly. —A STORM OF SWORDS

Medieval Cream of Mushroom and Snail Soup

Serves 4 + Prep: 5 minutes + Cooking: 25 minutes

*Pairs well with Medieval Pease Porridge (page 38),
Crusty White Bread (page 25), white wine*

This dish is very different from modern soups, and typically medieval in its flavors. The almond milk in the broth and strong spices such as clove and mace give the soup a character all its own. While intended to be made with oysters, the original recipe brilliantly accommodates the substitution of escargots.

Oystres en grauey.—Take gode Mylke of Almaundys, an drawe it wyth Wyne an gode Fysshe broþe, an sette it on þe fyre, & let boyle; & caste þer-to Clowes, Maces, Sugre an powder Gyngere, an a fewe parboylid Oynonys y-mynsyd; þan take fayre Oystrys, & parboyle hem in fayre Water, & caste hem þer-to, an lete hem boyle to-gederys; & þanne serue hem forth.

—TWO FIFTEENTH-CENTURY COOKERY-BOOKS

2 tablespoons unsalted butter

1 medium onion, minced

½ cup white wine

½ cup fish stock

1 cup small mushrooms or roughly chopped larger mushrooms

1 tablespoon sugar

1½ cups almond milk

1 cup fresh or canned escargots

Pinch of ground ginger

Pinch of ground cloves

Pinch of mace

Melt the butter in a saucepan over medium heat and sauté the onion until the pieces are soft, about 5 minutes.

In a separate pot, combine the wine and fish stock, bring the mixture to a boil, and add the mushrooms. Turn down the heat to low, cover the pot, and simmer for 10 minutes.

Add the sugar and almond milk to the pot with the wine and stock, keeping the mixture hot but not boiling. Add the escargots and cooked onions, followed by spices to taste.

Bring to a boil, stirring constantly, until the soup has thickened slightly. Serve hot.

Modern Cream of Mushroom and Snail Soup

Serves 4 + Prep: 10 minutes + Cooking: 30 minutes

*Pairs well with Crusty White Bread (page 25),
Summer Greens Salad (page 133), Tyroshi Pear Brandy (page 211)*

An inherently rich, flavorful dish, this soup is divine. The creamy texture of the escargot is countered nicely by the fresh, clean taste of parsley. The wine in the broth adds a depth of flavor, and the longer the broth is cooked down, the creamier and more decadent it becomes. It also makes for fantastic leftovers!

2½ cups chopped mushrooms: a mix of chanterelle, oyster, and shiitake

1 small onion, chopped

4 cups chicken stock

6 tablespoons unsalted butter

¼ cup flour

1 cup whole or part-skimmed milk

1 cup light cream

Salt and pepper to taste

One 6-ounce can escargots, drained and chopped

2 garlic cloves, minced

¼ cup chopped parsley

2 green onions, chopped

¼ cup white wine

Combine the mushrooms, onion, and chicken stock in a saucepan and simmer for 20 minutes.

In a separate pot, melt 4 tablespoons of the butter over medium heat and stir in the flour; cook until the mixture turns a nice golden color. Add the milk and cream, stirring constantly until smooth. Season with salt and pepper, then stir in the mushroom and chicken stock.

Sauté the escargots, garlic, parsley, and green onions in the remaining 2 tablespoons of butter for about 2 minutes, then add them to the soup, along with the wine. Serve hot.

Sweet Pumpkin Soup

Her father had been fighting with the council again. Arya could see it on his face when he came to table, late again, as he had been so often. The first course, a thick sweet soup made with pumpkins, had already been taken away when Ned Stark strode into the Small Hall.

—A GAME OF THRONES

**Serves 4 to 6 ✦ Roasting vegetables: 1½ hours
Cooking: 10 minutes**

*Pairs well with Black Bread (page 85),
Sweetcorn Fritters (page 123), Modern Honey Biscuits (page 115)*

Although served in the capital of King's Landing, this is every bit a Northern autumnal soup. Sweetened by yams, the bisque pairs butternut squash and pumpkin to perfection. Roasting the vegetables caramelizes them slightly, really bringing out the best of their innate flavors. Add a few dashes of spice, and you have a soup that Arya would rather eat than fling at her sister.

1 sugar pumpkin (around 4 pounds)	½ cup apple cider
1 large yam	2 cups chicken broth
½ medium butternut squash (cut lengthwise), seeds removed	½ teaspoon ground nutmeg
	1 teaspoon ground ginger
	1 teaspoon ground cinnamon

Preheat the oven to 350°F.

Using a sharp knife, cut the pumpkin in half horizontally. Clean out the inside, removing all the stringy innards and seeds. (You can roast the seeds, making them into a lovely snack for later.)

Wrap the yam in foil and place it on a baking sheet along with the butternut squash half and the two pumpkin halves. Roast all the vegetables until they are soft, about 1½ hours.

Mash the yam, the squash, and the flesh from the pumpkin together in a large saucepan. Add the cider, broth, and spices, and blend either in an upright blender, or using an immersion blender. Return the soup to the pan and heat until it is hot through.

Summer Greens Salad

This evening they had supped on oxtail soup, summer greens tossed with pecans, grapes, red fennel, and crumbled cheese, hot crab pie, spiced squash, and quails drowned in butter. Lord Janos allowed that he had never eaten half so well. —A CLASH OF KINGS

Serves 6 ✦ Prep: 15 minutes

Pairs well with Fish Tarts (page 140),
Modern Stewed Rabbit (page 96), Apricot Tarts (page 162)

The varied flavors and textures of this salad make for a taste that is both complex and sophisticated. The sweetness of grapes and apricot counters the tang of the arugula, while the bite of the fennel gives a flavor that lingers on the tongue. The combination of nuts, crunchy fennel, gooey jam, and firm grapes will give your palate a great deal to experience.

1 fennel bulb	5 ounces arugula (lightly packed, stemmed, 8 cups)
4 teaspoons apricot jam	
3 tablespoons white wine vinegar	1 cup seedless grapes (red or green), halved
3 tablespoons extra-virgin olive oil	
	¾ cup crumbled gorgonzola
1 shallot, minced	½ cup chopped pecans (the candied version is wonderful)
Salt and ground black pepper	

Cut the fennel in half lengthwise and reserve one part for another use. Trim the stalks from the remaining half bulb, core it, and slice it very thin; set aside. Trim the fennel fronds from the stalks and set them aside; discard the stalks.

Whisk the jam, vinegar, oil, shallot, and ¼ teaspoon each salt and pepper together in a large bowl.

Toss the fennel slices with the vinaigrette; let them stand for 15 minutes.

Add the arugula, fennel fronds, and grapes; toss, and adjust the seasonings with salt and pepper.

Top with gorgonzola and pecans and serve.

Sansa Salad

All the while the courses came and went. A thick soup of barley and venison. Salads of sweetgrass, spinach, and plums, sprinkled with crushed nuts. —A GAME OF THRONES

Serves 4 to 6 + Prep: 10 minutes

Pairs well with Pigeon Pie (page 147),
Honeyed Chicken (page 77), plum wine

This is a tasty, tasty salad, based loosely on instructions for making a salad from the 14th-century *Forme of Cury*. All the elements work beautifully with one another both texturally and aesthetically. Pack this for a lunch or serve it as a light afternoon meal, and you won't be disappointed.

Salat. Take persel, sawge, grene garlec, chibolles, letys, leek, spinoches, borage, myntes, prymos, violettes, porrettes, fenel, and toun cressis, rosemarye, purslarye; laue and waishe hem clene. Pike hem. Pluk hem small wiþ þyn honde, and myng hem wel with rawe oile; lay on vyneger and salt, and serue it forth.

—THE FORME OF CURY, 14TH CENTURY

7 cups baby spinach

1 cup fresh mint leaves

1 cup diced prunes

½ cup candied walnuts

½ cup fresh lemongrass, thinly
    sliced

½ cup violets, primroses, or other
    edible flowers (optional)

raspberry vinaigrette to taste

Combine the spinach, mint, prunes, walnuts, and lemongrass in a large bowl. The edible flowers can be mixed in with the salad at this point or used as a garnish on top. Pour the vinaigrette over all, then toss well and serve.

+ **Cook's Note:** Use this recipe as a starting point and choose any variation of these ingredients—or others—to create your own personal "salat." Toss with dressing, and you're ready to serve!

Buttered Carrots

Cersei set a tasty table, that could not be denied. They started with a creamy chestnut soup, crusty hot bread, and greens dressed with apples and pine nuts. Then came lamprey pie, honeyed ham, buttered carrots, white beans and bacon, and roast swan stuffed with mushrooms and oysters. —A CLASH OF KINGS

Roman Buttered Carrots

Serves 2 to 4 ✦ Prep: 10 minutes ✦ Cooking: 20 minutes

Pairs well with Honeyed Chicken (page 77), White Beans and Bacon (page 149), sweet red wine

We tweaked the ancient recipes a bit. We swapped butter for olive oil, added raisins to the carrot dish, and left out the fish sauce because of personal preference, but feel free to include a dash of it if you'd like. The resulting dish is a unique approach to cooked carrots that falls somewhere between sweet and savory.

Aliter: caroetas elixatas concisas in cuminato oleo modico coques et inferes. cuminatum colourium facies.

Cuminatum in ostrea et conchylia: Piper, ligusticum, petroselinum, mentam siccam, cuminum plusculum, mel, acetum et liquamen. —APICIUS, 4TH CENTURY

2 cups chopped carrots (use
    heirloom carrots, if available)
½ cup raisins
2 to 3 tablespoons honey

2 tablespoons wine vinegar
2 teaspoons cumin (roasted and
    ground seed is best, but the
    powder works well)

Ground black pepper to taste
2 tablespoons melted unsalted
   butter

2 tablespoons sweet wine,
   red or white

Preheat the oven to 400°F.

Cut the carrots into disks or chunks. Put them in a pot of water and bring it to a boil, then drain them immediately and place them in an ovenproof dish. Add the raisins, honey, vinegar, cumin, and pepper. Drizzle the butter over top, then shake well to coat the carrots, and roast until they are tender. Add the wine to deglaze the sticky pan and dislodge the carrots, then pour the whole contents of the pan into a serving dish. Serve warm.

Modern Buttered Carrots

Serves 6 ✦ Prep: 10 minutes ✦ Cooking: 25 minutes

Pairs well with Beef and Bacon Pie (page 71),
Summer Greens Salad (page 133), white wine

3 tablespoons unsalted butter

2 pounds carrots, peeled and cut
　　diagonally into ¼-inch slices

Kosher salt

Ground black pepper

2 tablespoons finely chopped fresh
　　chives or scallions

Melt the butter in a large skillet over medium heat. Add the carrots and ½ teaspoon salt and cook, covered, until steam begins to escape from under the lid, about 5 minutes. Reduce the heat to low and continue to cook, covered and stirring occasionally, until the carrots are just tender, 15 to 20 minutes.

Remove the lid, add ¼ teaspoon pepper, and cook, stirring occasionally, until the liquid is evaporated and the butter begins to brown, about 5 more minutes. Sprinkle with chives and season with more salt and pepper if needed. Serve.

Fish Tarts

Their feats were accompanied by crabs boiled in fiery eastern spices, tren-chers filled with chunks of chopped mutton stewed in almond milk with carrots, raisins, and onions, and fish tarts fresh from the ovens, served so hot they burned the fingers. —A STORM OF SWORDS

Medieval Fish Tarts

Makes about 1 dozen mini tarts ✦ Prep: 15 minutes
Cooking: 15 minutes

Pairs well with Sister's Stew (page 90),
Almond Crusted Trout (page 156), sweet red wine

These make great appetizers for a fish-based dinner. This medieval interpretation is a pleasing blend of sweet and savory flavors. The figs add an interesting texture and act as the base for the filling, while the dates increase the sweetness to a satisfying level without the addition of processed sugar.

Tartes of Frute in lente.—Take Fygys & sethe hem wyl tyl þey ben neyssche; þan bray hem in a morter, & a pece of Milwel þer-with; take ham vppe & caste roysonys of coraunce þer-to; þan take Almaundys & Dates y-schred þer-to; þan take pouder of Pepir & meng with-al; þen putte it on þin cofynne, & Safroun þin cofynn a-boue, & opyn hem a-bowte þe myddel; & ouer-cast þe openyng vppon þe lede, & bake hym a lytel, & serue forth.

— TWO FIFTEENTH-CENTURY COOKERY-BOOKS

¼ pound salmon fillet
1 pint fresh figs (about 1½ cups)
¼ cup slivered or sliced almonds
6 dates, pitted and quartered

½ batch Medieval Pastry Dough
  (see page 9) or 12 premade
  mini tart shells

Preheat the oven to 375°F.

If using homemade pastry dough, roll out to ¼-inch thickness. Cut 1-inch circles with a cookie cutter, and press into a mini cupcake pan, or mini-tartlette or brioche molds.

Add the salmon to a pot of simmering water, and poach for about 4 minutes, or until cooked through. Set it aside to cool.

Boil the figs for 10 minutes, or until tender. Drain and place them in a mixing bowl. Add the almonds and dates. Shred the fish and take care to remove any bones; add it to the bowl with the fruit and nuts. Mix the ingredients thoroughly, and spoon the filling into the pastry shells.

Bake for 15 minutes, or until the pastry is golden and the filling is beginning to crisp. Serve immediately while still warm.

Modern Fish Tarts

Makes about 24 mini tarts + Prep: 10 minutes + Cooking: 20 minutes

Pairs well with Cheese-and-Onion Pie (page 143),
Sister's Stew (page 90), white wine

Like the medieval tarts, these make great appetizers. The cream-cheese filling is delectable—with the smoked fish, it feels like eating a well-crafted bagel. The sage

adds a great kick and an additional layer to the flavor. If you have extra filling, save it to use as a spread for crackers and bread!

1 sheet puff pastry or 24 mini tart shells

8 ounces smoked fish of your choice (we used trout)

16 ounces cream cheese

2 ounces heavy cream

2 tablespoons chopped fresh sage

½ pint blackberries

Preheat the oven to 375°F.

Break the fish into small chunks. Mix together the cream cheese, cream, sage, and smoked fish. If using puff pastry, roll it out as thin as you can and cut it into 3-inch circles.

Scoop up 1 tablespoon of the cream cheese mixture and form it into a roughly round shape; place it in the middle of a pastry circle and wrap the sides around the filling (or place the filling in the premade pastry shell). Press a blackberry onto the top of each tart. Bake for 20 minutes, or until the pastry is golden and the blackberries have darkened. Serve immediately.

Cheese-and-Onion Pie

Moon Boy mounted his stilts and strode around the tables in pursuit of Lord Tyrell's ludicrously fat fool Butterbumps, and the lords and ladies sampled roast herons and cheese-and-onion pies. —A STORM OF SWORDS

Medieval Cheese-and-Onion Pie

Serves 6 to 8 ✦ Prep: 15 minutes ✦ Baking: 30 to 45 minutes

Pairs well with Aurochs Roasted with Leeks (page 75),
White Beans and Bacon (page 149), dry white wine

This makes a quirky quiche-like pie, in which the basil and fruit are the stars. The currants are a surprising and pleasant sweetness at the end of every bite. The pie is delicious on its own and nicely accompanies any sort of roasted meat.

Tart in ymbre day. Take and þboile oynons psse out þ wat & hewe he smale. Take brede & bray it i a mort, and temp it up w ayren. Do þto butt, safron and salt, & raisons corans, & a litel sug with powdo douce, and bake it i a trap, & sue it forth. —THE FORME OF CURY, 14TH CENTURY

½ batch Medieval Pastry Dough
    (see page 9), unbaked
3 to 4 medium onions, finely
    chopped or thinly sliced
Fresh herbs, 1 sprig each sage,
    basil, and thyme
¼ cup dried currants
2 tablespoons flour
1 grated cup of your favorite
    creamy cheese, such as Havarti
    or Muenster

8 eggs, beaten
1 tablespoon unsalted butter,
    melted
¼ teaspoon saffron
½ teaspoon salt
1 teaspoon Poudre Douce (see
    page 5)

Preheat the oven to 350°F.

Roll out the pastry dough, fit it into the bottom of a pie or quiche pan, and set it aside.

Parboil the onions and herbs for 5 minutes, then drain them well. Press the herbs dry and chop them finely. Toss the currants with flour; this will keep them from sinking to the bottom of the pie.

Combine the onions, herbs, currants, cheese, eggs, butter, saffron, salt, and poudre douce in a bowl. Mix them thoroughly and pour the filling into the prepared pastry shell.

Bake for 30 to 45 minutes, or until the pastry dough is browned. Remove from oven, and serve while still warm.

Modern Cheese-and-Onion Pie

Serves 6 to 8 ✦ Prep: 15 minutes ✦ Baking: 35 to 45 minutes

Pairs well with Pease Porridge (page 38),
Modern Honey Biscuits (page 115), Iced Milk with Honey (page 169)

If you are looking for a hearty winter meal to warm your insides and stick to your ribs, this is the recipe. Based on a British recipe, this pie is both creamy and heavy. It has an *au gratin* feel, but serves as either a side dish or a meal unto itself.

2 medium potatoes, peeled and
  cut into small cubes
2 onions, finely chopped
1 tablespoon flour

¼ cup whole milk
¼ cup heavy cream
1½ cups grated aged cheddar
  cheese

½ teaspoon English
mustard

½ teaspoon cayenne pepper

Salt and pepper to taste

1 batch Medieval Pastry Dough
(see page 9), unbaked, rolled
into 2 rounds

1 egg white for glaze (optional)

Preheat the oven to 350°F.

Boil the potatoes in salted water for 10 to 15 minutes, then drain and set them aside.

Boil the chopped onions in salted water for 2 to 3 minutes, then drain and return them to the saucepan. Coat the onions with the flour, then add the milk and cream to the saucepan. Cook over medium heat, stirring continuously, for 3 or 4 minutes, until the liquid is smooth and slightly thickened. Add the potatoes, cheese, mustard, and cayenne; stir well. Season with salt and pepper.

Grease a pie tin and line the base and sides with a round of dough. Prick the base of the pastry several times with a fork. Pour the pie filling into the pastry shell. Brush the rim of the pastry shell with beaten egg or water and place the second pastry round onto the pie. Trim the excess pastry and crimp the edges with a fork to seal. Make four small holes in the center of the pastry lid and brush with the remaining egg white, if using.

Bake for 35 to 45 minutes, or until golden brown. Remove from oven and allow to cool to just above room temperature before serving.

Pigeon Pie

"My uncle hasn't eaten his pigeon pie." Holding the chalice one-handed,
Joff jammed his other into Tyrion's pie. *"It's ill luck not to eat the pie. . . ."*

—A STORM OF SWORDS

Serves 6 to 8 ✦ Prep: 1½ hours ✦ Baking: 30 minutes

Pairs well with Buttered Carrots (page 137),
Sweet Pumpkin Soup (page 131), red wine

Pigeon meat is dark, like duck, although not nearly as fatty. The silky texture of the meat is the real showstopper—wonderfully soft and tender, complementing the light, flaky pastry crust. Although we used the suggested spices from a medieval pigeon pie recipe, we made ours with vegetables too, much like a chicken pot pie, so it oozes with vegetables and a creamy sauce. Because of the richness of the pigeon, a small slice will satisfy, and it's best paired with an assortment of sides.

Season your pigeons with peper saffron cloves and mace with vergis and salt then
put them into your paest and so close them vp and bake them these will bake in
halfe an houre then take them forth and if ye thynke them drye take a litle vergis
and butter and put to them and so serue them.

—A PROPRE NEW BOOKE OF COKERY, 1545

5 pigeons, cleaned and dressed

A few fresh cloves

2 tablespoons unsalted butter

2 leeks (white and light green
    parts only), well washed and
    thinly sliced

1 medium turnip, diced (about 1½
    cups total)

½ cup sliced mushrooms

Roux (see page 8)

1 cup chicken stock

4 tablespoons heavy cream

1 teaspoon mace

Salt and ground black pepper
    to taste

1 batch Medieval Pastry Dough (see page 9), unbaked, rolled into 2 rounds

Beaten egg for glaze (optional)

Put the pigeons in a large pot and just cover them with water. Throw in the cloves, simmer for around 45 minutes, and drain, reserving the broth. Pluck the meat from the breasts. Cut it into long strips and set it aside. (There is so little meat on the rest of the pigeon that the carcasses can be discarded after this.)

Preheat the oven to 375°F.

In a skillet, melt the butter and sauté the leeks until they are soft, but not brown. Add the turnip and mushrooms and stir until the pieces are all coated in butter. Add a splash of the reserved pigeon broth, then cover and simmer until the turnips are soft.

Make the roux, then pour in the chicken stock. Cook for 2 to 3 minutes, until the mixture has thickened and is smooth. Whisk in the cream, mace, and salt and pepper. Pour your cooked vegetables and pigeon meat into this creamy sauce and stir well.

Grease a pie tin and line the base and sides with a round of pastry dough. Prick the base of the pastry several times with a fork. Pour the filling into the pastry shell. Brush the rim of it with beaten egg or water, and place the second pastry round onto the pie. Trim the excess pastry and crimp the edges with a fork to seal. Make four small holes in the center of the pastry lid and brush with the remaining egg, if using. Bake for around 30 minutes, or until the crust is golden.

White Beans and Bacon

Then came lamprey pie, honeyed ham, buttered carrots, white beans and bacon, and roast swan stuffed with mushrooms and oysters.

—A CLASH OF KINGS

Medieval White Beans and Bacon

Serves 4 to 6   +   Soaking beans: overnight
Prep: 5 to 10 minutes   +   Cooking: 15 minutes

Pairs well with Rack of Lamb (page 42),
Black Bread (page 85), dark beer

Roughly chopped lardons paired with the buttery beans make for a lovely mouthful—the beans really soak up the flavor of the bacon. The onions offer a bit of caramelized sweetness at the end of every bite.

*Benes yfryed. Take benes and seeþ he almost til þey bersten. Take and wryng out
þ wat clene. Do þto oynons ysode and ymynced, and garlec þw; frye hem i oile oþ
i grece, & do þto powdo douce, & sue it forth.*

—THE FORME OF CURY, 14TH CENTURY

4 slices bacon, roughly chopped

1 cup dried white beans, soaked
  overnight, or one 16-ounce can
  white beans

1 small onion, minced

1 clove garlic, minced

½ teaspoon Poudre Douce (see
  page 5)

Cook the bacon in a large skillet over medium-high heat. When it is done to your
taste, transfer it to a separate plate, leaving the bacon grease in the pan. Sauté the
onion and garlic in the bacon drippings until soft.

Turn down the heat to medium and add the bacon, beans, and spices to the onions. Stir until all ingredients are hot. Serve immediately.

+ *Tip:* For a slightly more modern twist, try seasoning this dish with a dash of
sambar powder and just a touch of sugar instead of the poudre douce.

Modern White Beans and Bacon

**Serves 6 to 8 + Soaking beans: overnight
Prep: 10 minutes + Cooking: 15 minutes**

Pairs well with Pork Pie (page 35), Modern Arya Tarts (page 102)

This dish is incredible. Curly endive is reminiscent of broccoli rabe; its slight bitterness is balanced phenomenally by the sweetness of the onions. The dish is quick to
prepare and can easily be scaled up for more people.

4 pieces bacon, roughly chopped

1 small onion, chopped

1 head curly endive, leaves rinsed
  and torn

2 large garlic cloves, chopped

1 cup dried white beans, soaked overnight, or one 16-ounce can white beans

Salt and ground black pepper to taste

Cook the bacon in a large saucepan over medium-high heat until crisp. Remove the bacon from the pan and set it on paper towels to drain. Add the onion to the drippings, and sauté until tender.

Add half the endive leaves and cover the pot, cooking until the endive is wilted, about 5 minutes. Add the remaining endive and the garlic, then cover and cook until the endive has wilted again.

Add the beans and bacon, cooking until the beans are heated through, stirring often. Season with salt and pepper and serve.

Bowls of Brown

In the Bottom there were pot-shops along the alleys where huge tubs of stew had been simmering for years . . . but the brown wasn't so bad. It usually had barley in it, and chunks of carrot and onion and turnip, and sometimes even apple, with a film of grease swimming on top.

—A GAME OF THRONES

Serves 10 to 12 ✦ Prep: 5 minutes ✦ Cooking: 8 hours

Pairs well with Black Bread (page 85), Tyroshi Honeyfingers (page 202), dark beer

For a truly authentic taste of Flea Bottom—the seething heart of King's Landing—one looks to the pot-shops. This recipe matches the original description, in that it is thick and full of a variety of meats and vegetables and, because it's intended for the poor, entirely without frills. It's more a curiosity than something to serve at a nice dinner party, but it could be dressed up to suit your tastes. (The optional seasonings at the end of the ingredients list may not all be available in King's Landing, but they will make Bowls of Brown far tastier.) Be innovative, and use whatever combination of meats you desire. Stirring up the pot to see what is on the bottom becomes a kind of adventure, as bones large and small turn up amid the barley and shreds of meat.

About 5 pounds mixed meat, for
    example:
2 pounds beef soup bones or ribs
2 cups cubed goat meat
1 pound top round steak, cut into
    small pieces
2 chicken thighs

1 whole game hen
3 cups dark beer
Beef broth
1 cup barley
2 apples, cored and chopped
1 cup pearl onions, peeled
2 carrots, cut into chunks

1 tablespoon salt	Flavoring such as liquid smoke,
2 teaspoons Poudre Forte (see page 6)	Worcestershire sauce, garlic, or molasses (optional)

This recipe is ideal for cooking in a slow cooker; you'll need the largest size insert available. Add all your meat to the pot. Pour in the beer, add beef broth to cover, and set the temperature to medium high. Let cook for about 6 hours. Add the barley, apple, pearl onions, carrots, and seasonings, continue to simmer for another two hours, and serve.

If you don't have a slow cooker, follow the above directions, using a large pot over medium heat. Adjust the burner temperature to ensure a slow, gentle simmer. Keep an eye on the level of liquid and add more if needed.

✦ *Tip:* If you find your stew isn't thickening satisfactorily, try adding a roux (see page 8).

✦ *Cook's Note:* If you are putting a whole bird into the pot, be sure to warn your guests about the possibility of small bones. When we served this, we turned the meal into a competition to see who had the most bones left in the bowl at the end, and named the winner "Rattleshirt."

Quails Drowned in Butter

This evening they had supped on oxtail soup, summer greens tossed with pecans, grapes, red fennel, and crumbled cheese, hot crab pie, spiced squash, and quails drowned in butter. Lord Janos allowed that he had never eaten half so well. —A CLASH OF KINGS

Serves 2 ✦ Prep: 15 minutes
Marinating: 1 hour or overnight ✦ Cooking: 10 to 15 minutes

Pairs well with Summer Greens Salad (page 133),
Turnips in Butter (page 68), red or white wine

This recipe is a bit labor-intensive, but the result is worth it. The apple slices sweeten the quail from the inside out, and the sauce is lovely and complex. When it comes to quail, there is only a small amount of meat on each bird, but it is rich, so your guests should be as well fed as they will be impressed by receiving two quails on their plates.

1 small apple, cored and quartered

4 whole quails

Elizabethan Butter Sauce (see page 7)

Unsalted butter

Salt and ground black pepper to taste

1 spoonful honey (optional)

Place a piece of apple inside the cavity of each quail. With the breast side up, fold the legs up and over toward the neck, and tie with string under the neck. Fold the wings around so the tips lie in between the trussed legs and the breast. This will keep them from burning. You may also truss the quail as you would a chicken or turkey.

Pour the Elizabethan Butter Sauce along with the quails into a large Ziploc bag. If you are doing this the day before serving, put the birds in the fridge to marinate overnight. Otherwise, leave the birds at room temperature for 1 hour.

When you are ready to cook, preheat the oven to 425°F.

Transfer the quails to a baking dish and place them breast side up. Rub the quails with the butter, salt, and pepper. Pour the butter sauce marinade into a frying pan and cook it over medium-high heat. Let it reduce until slightly thickened, 5 to 10 minutes. You can add a little honey if you want to increase the syrupy consistency.

When the marinade has reduced, brush the quails with the sauce. Bake for about 10 minutes, or until the juices run yellow.

+ *Cook's Note:* Consider serving the dish with white wine in summer and red in winter.

Almond Crusted Trout

Hamish left them, his place taken by a smallish elderly bear who danced clumsily to pipe and drum while the wedding guests ate trout in a crust of crushed almonds. —A STORM OF SWORDS

Serves 2 ✦ Prep: 15 minutes ✦ Grilling: 1 hour

Pairs well with Modern White Beans and Bacon (page 150), Medieval Armored Turnips (page 68), white wine

The crust, which doubles as an awesome stuffing, has a sweetness reminiscent of other sweet-savory medieval recipes, with the almonds and lemon really punching through. It helps keep the fish moist and tender, flaking off the bone. We made this recipe with whole fish, but it's also great for fillets. The key is to cook it slowly at a low heat, to ensure that the crust doesn't burn and the fish doesn't dry out.

¼ cup fresh parsley, chopped

¼ cup fresh dill, chopped

2 shallots, chopped

½ cup chopped or ground almonds (we chopped almonds, then pounded them with a mortar and pestle)

1 teaspoon salt

¼ cup bread crumbs

4 cloves garlic, minced

¼ cup lemon juice

1 egg

½ cup flour

2 small cleaned and gutted trout, or 4 trout fillets

Heat a grill to low or preheat the oven to 275°F.

Mix the herbs, shallots, almonds, salt, and bread crumbs together by hand or in a food processor. Add in the garlic, lemon juice, and egg and mix until uniform in texture. Put the flour into a shallow bowl and dredge the fish in the flour. Gently pack the almond mixture inside and around the fish. Grill or bake for about 1 hour, or until the crust is just crispy and the fish is cooked through. Plate and serve.

Roasted Boar

"Sansa," Lady Alerie broke in, "you must be very hungry. Shall we have a bite of boar together, and some lemon cakes?" —A STORM OF SWORDS

Serves 2 + Prep: 15 minutes
Marinating: 1 hour or overnight + Roasting: 15 to 25 minutes
Sauce: 15 minutes

Pairs well with Oatbread (page 125), Sweetcorn Fritters (page 123), mead

At first quite peppery, the sauce quickly mellows into a complex medley of flavors that delights the palate. Cloves are predominant, but despite the quantity, the flavor isn't overwhelming. The boar itself is like a delicious hybrid—the texture similar to a high-quality cut of steak, and the richness like venison, but without the accompanying gaminess. A medieval must!

Primo le convient mettre en eaue boulant, et bien tost retraire et boutonner de giroffle; mettre rostir, et baciner de sausse faicte d'espices, c'est assavoir gingembre, canelle, giroffle, graine, poivre long et noix muguettes, destrempé de vertjus, vin et vinaigre, et sans boulir l'en baciner; et quant il sera rosti, si boulez tout ensemble. Et ceste sausse est appellée queue de sanglier, et la trouverez cy-après

—LE MENAGIER DE PARIS, 1393

4 boar tenderloins, about
    ¼ pound each
⅔ cup red wine, such as a
    rioja or Syrah
⅔ cup red wine vinegar

1 cup apple cider or white
    grape juice
2 teaspoons Poudre Forte (see
    page 6)
12 to 20 whole cloves

Place the boar tenderloins in a Ziploc bag or a baking dish. Mix the wine, vinegar, and juice with 1 teaspoon of the poudre forte, and pour the marinade over the boar. Allow the meat to sit in the fridge for several hours or overnight.

Preheat the oven to 350°F.

Drain the liquid into a saucepan, and set it aside. Using a sharp paring knife, make small holes in the tenderloins and insert whole cloves into the meat; 3 to 5 cloves per tenderloin should suffice. Sprinkle the remaining 1 teaspoon poudre forte over the tenderloins, pressing the spices into the meat.

Line a baking pan with tinfoil and place the boar on it. Roast the meat for 15 minutes, then check for doneness. Depending on the size of your tenderloins, it may take up to 10 minutes longer.

Remove the boar from the oven and pour any juices from the baking pan into the reserved marinade. Cover the boar to keep it warm.

Simmer the sauce ingredients until they have reduced slightly, around 15 minutes. Pour the sauce over the boar and serve.

Peaches in Honey

*When a serving girl brought [Sansa] her supper, she almost kissed her.
There was hot bread and fresh-churned butter, a thick beef soup, capon
and carrots, and peaches in honey.* Even the food tastes sweeter, *she
thought.* —A CLASH OF KINGS

Roman Peaches in Honey-Cumin Sauce

Serves 8 or more ✦ Prep: 15 minutes ✦ Baking: 30 minutes

*Pairs well with Pork Pie (page 35),
Honeyed Chicken (page 77), Sansa Salad (page 135), sweet wine*

This is a curious recipe, taken from an ancient Roman text on cookery. The combination of pepper, cumin, and fruit turns familiar flavors into something unusual, each element lingering in its turn on the palate. The dish would work beautifully as a chutney or as a side dish to a meaty main course—it isn't what most of us consider a dessert. A little bit goes a long way, but this is what your favorite meat course didn't know it was missing.

> *Persica duriora purgabis, frustratim concides, elixas, in patina compones, olei modicum superstillabis et cum cuminato inferes.* —APICIUS, 4TH CENTURY

1 teaspoon ground cumin

½ teaspoon ground white pepper

¼ cup honey

¼ cup white wine vinegar

Pinch of dried mint

4 peaches, ripe or just underripe

2 tablespoons olive oil

Preheat oven to 350°F.

Roast the cumin in a dry pan until it turns fragrant and just begins to darken; this takes only a few minutes. Mix the roasted cumin with the pepper and set aside.

Mix the honey and vinegar in a saucepan, then cook it over medium heat until the honey has melted into the vinegar. Stir in the spice mix and the mint. Simmer briefly, stirring, until everything is combined.

Peel the peaches, remove the pits, and cut them into slices. Place the peach slices in a large baking pan and toss them with olive oil. Pour the cumin sauce over the peaches and bake for 30 minutes.

Modern Grilled Peaches in Honey

Serves 8 ✦ Prep: 5 minutes
Grilling: 8 to 10 minutes ✦ Honey glaze: 30 minutes

Pairs well with Modern Bean-and-Bacon Soup (page 31),
Beef and Bacon Pie (page 71), white wine

These peaches are pure deliciousness. Grilling brings out the fullness of the peach flavors, and they become reminiscent of peach pie filling. The thyme-infused honey takes the sweetness and complexity to the next level. You will want to savor every single bite. Consider adding a dollop of crème fraîche or vanilla ice cream to complete the dish.

3 tablespoons honey

2 tablespoons lemon juice

3 fresh thyme sprigs, plus more for garnish if desired

4 firm ripe peaches, cut in half, pits discarded

1 tablespoon vegetable oil

Mascarpone, crème fraîche, or vanilla ice cream for serving

Chopped nuts for garnish (optional)

In a small pot, whisk together the honey and lemon juice. Add the thyme sprigs and cook over low heat for 3 minutes, stirring constantly. Remove the pan from the heat, cover it, and let the mixture steep for 15 to 20 minutes. Then discard thyme sprigs and strain the glaze if necessary. You can serve it cold or reheat it when the peaches are ready.

Shortly before you are ready to serve the dessert, put the peach halves in a bowl, drizzle them with oil, and mix them with your hands. Make sure all the peaches are coated with a thin layer of oil. Heat a grill pan.

Put the peaches on the hot pan, cut-side down. Cook them for 4 to 5 minutes, then turn them over. Cook for another 4 minutes, or until the peaches are soft but still firm (they shouldn't fall apart).

Place the peaches on plates, drizzle them with glaze, and top with a dollop of mascarpone, crème fraîche, or a scoop of ice cream. Decorate with chopped nuts or thyme sprigs.

Apricot Tarts

A man was pushing a load of tarts by on a two-wheeled cart; the smells
sang of blueberries and lemons and apricots. [Arya's] stomach made a
hollow rumbly noise. "Could I have one?" she heard herself say.

—A GAME OF THRONES

Medieval Apricot Tarts

Makes eight 4-inch tarts or one 9-inch tart
Prep: 15 minutes + Baking: 45 minutes

Pairs well with Almond Crusted Trout (page 156),
Salad at Castle Black (page 27), semisweet white wine

The original 14th-century recipe for this tart includes several different kinds of fruit
but is still delicious when altered to showcase apricots. The yellow-orange of the
apricots is beautiful against the red of the sandalwood-tinted creamy filling, and the
combination of fresh and dried fruit creates a textural balance.

Lesshes fryed in lenton. Drawe a thick almande mylke wiþ wat. Take dat and pyke
he clene w apples and peere & mynce he w pnes&; take out þ ston out of þ pnes,
& kerue the pnes a two. Do þto raisons, sug, flo of canel, hoole macys and clow,
gode powdos & salt; colo hem vp with sandr. Meng þise with oile. Make a coffyn
as þ didest bifor & do þis fars þin, & bake it wel, and sue it forth.

—THE FORME OF CURY, 14TH CENTURY

2 cups almond milk

2 tablespoons sugar

½ teaspoon ground cinnamon

½ teaspoon ground mace

½ teaspoon ground cloves

¼ teaspoon ground ginger

¼ teaspoon ground nutmeg

¼ teaspoon ground white pepper

¼ teaspoon salt

2 tablespoons olive oil

1 tablespoon sandalwood powder, or a few drops of red food coloring

½ cup dried apricots, sliced into thin strips

3 to 5 fresh apricots, diced

½ cup pitted prunes, thinly sliced lengthwise

½ cup currants

1 batch Medieval Pastry Dough (see page 9), prebaked into one 9-inch shell or eight 4-inch shells

Preheat oven to 375°F.

Mix together the almond milk, sugar, spices, pepper, salt, oil, and sandalwood. The color should be a brilliant red, and the mixture should be thick but runny.

In a separate bowl, combine the fruits. Spread the fruit mixture into the shell, then spoon the almond milk mixture over it.

Bake for 45 minutes, or until the filling is set and the top has slightly browned. Allow the tart to cool completely before serving.

Modern Apricot Tarts

Makes 4 small tarts + Prep: 15 minutes + Baking: 25 to 30 minutes

Pairs well with Quails Drowned in Butter (page 154),
Sansa Salad (page 135), dry white wine

This dessert is beautiful in presentation and has a more delicate taste than tarts that use dried apricots. The fresh fruit is lighter and is accented by the combination of lemon and pistachio.

1 batch Lemon Pastry Dough (see page 10)

5 fresh apricots

4 teaspoons sugar

1 teaspoon chopped pistachios

¼ cup tart cherry juice (optional)

Preheat the oven to 350°F.

Divide the dough into 4 equal parts. Roll out each piece and press it into a 4-inch tartlet pan.

Cut the apricots into very thin wedges and arrange them in the tart pans, starting from the outside and working in; place the slices curved side up. Sprinkle each tart with 1 teaspoon sugar and some chopped pistachios. Bake for 25 to 30 minutes, or until the pastry is golden brown. Allow the tarts to cool completely before removing them from the pans.

If desired, drizzle 1 tablespoon cherry juice over the top of each tart to add color and sweetness.

Lemon Cakes

Later came sweetbreads and pigeon pie and baked apples fragrant with cinnamon and lemon cakes frosted in sugar, but by then Sansa was so stuffed that she could not manage more than two little lemon cakes, as much as she loved them. —A GAME OF THRONES

Elizabethan Lemon Cakes

Makes 36 small cakes ✦ **Prep: 5 minutes** ✦ **Baking: 15 minutes**

Pairs well with Roasted Boar (page 157), Leek Soup (page 87), Iced Green Minty Drink (page 213)

Falling somewhere between cakes and cookies, these chewy lemon delights are both addictive and easy to make. They have an elegant simplicity and a delicate sweetness that renders them the ideal companions for afternoon tea, whether in London or King's Landing.

To Make Lemon Cakes. ½ lb flour, ½ lb fine sugar, the peel of two lemons, or one large one; 3 oz. butter; 3 eggs; ½ the whites. Break the butter into the flour and stir them with a knife. Make them the bigness of a gingerbread button. Grate the lemon peel with a piece of the sugar. Butter the tins. Take them of the tins whilst warm. Place them upon the tins about 2 inches distance because they spread in the oven. Two minutes will bake them. —LUCAYOS COOKBOOK, 1690

2½ cups flour, plus more as needed	1 egg
2 cups granulated sugar	2 egg yolks
6 tablespoons unsalted butter	⅓ cup confectioners' sugar
Grated zest from 2 lemons	1½ teaspoons milk

Preheat the oven to 350°F and grease a large baking sheet.

In a large bowl, combine the flour and granulated sugar. Cut in the butter, then add the zest and the whole egg and yolks. Mix thoroughly, adding more flour as needed, until the dough is no longer sticky and can be easily shaped by hand.*

Roll the dough into balls about 1 inch across and place them on the prepared baking sheet at least 2 inches apart, giving them room to spread as they bake.

Bake for 15 minutes, until the tops are just slightly golden. Allow the cakes to cool for a minute before moving them to a cooling rack.

Mix the confectioners' sugar and milk to a smooth consistency. Once the cakes have cooled, use a spoon to drizzle the icing over the cookies.

*If the mixture seems too dry, add a little water or lemon juice until the dough comes together.

Modern Lemon Cakes

Makes 45 to 60 mini cakes
Prep: 15 minutes + Baking: 30 minutes + Icing: 20 minutes

Pairs well with everything

Similar to French petit fours, these modern lemon cakes are just as addictive as the cakes produced by the Elizabethan recipe, but are sweeter and heavier than their historical counterparts.

For the Cake:

2½ cups all-purpose flour, well leveled

1½ teaspoons baking powder

¼ teaspoon baking soda

½ teaspoon salt

1 cup (2 sticks) unsalted butter, at room temperature, plus more for the pan

1½ cups sugar

2 teaspoons pure vanilla extract

3 large eggs, at room temperature

Juice from ½ lemon

2 to 4 tablespoons grated lemon zest

1 cup whole milk

For the Icing:

3 cups confectioners' sugar, sifted

⅓ cup lemon juice, plus more if needed

1 teaspoon unsalted butter, softened

Yellow food coloring (optional)

Garnishes such as candied orange peel, pomegranate seeds, or decorative sprinkles (optional)

Preheat the oven to 350°F. Butter the bottom of an 11-by-7-inch baking pan, line the bottom with parchment, butter again, and dust with flour; tap out any extra flour.

In a medium bowl, whisk together the flour, baking powder, baking soda, and salt; set aside.

In another bowl, using an electric mixer, beat the butter and sugar until fluffy. Add the vanilla, then the eggs one at a time, scraping down the sides of the bowl. Add lemon juice and lemon zest, mixing until just combined. Reduce the mixer speed to low. Add the flour mixture in three batches and the milk in two, beginning and ending with the flour mixture. Don't overmix!

Pour the batter into the prepared pan and bake for approximately 30 minutes, or until a toothpick inserted in the center comes out clean. The top of the cake should be just turning golden. Cool the cake in the pan for 15 minutes, then turn it out and cool it for another 15 minutes. Place the cake in refrigerator for at least 30 minutes.

Cut the chilled cake into cubes and set them aside. It's now time for the icing!

Mix the confectioners' sugar and lemon juice together in a double boiler over medium heat, stirring all the while. Stir in the butter. Mix until the icing is a nice, smooth consistency, suitable for pouring. Add more juice, if necessary. If you would like, tint the icing yellow with food coloring.

Drizzle icing over each cube of cake, making sure to cover the sides. Coat the cake only once, then let it cool for a minute. If desired, garnish with a piece of candied orange peel, a pomegranate seed, or decorative sprinkles. Let the icing cool completely and set before moving or serving the cakes.

Iced Milk with Honey

"Would you care for refreshments? Some dates, perhaps? I have some very fine persimmons as well. Wine no longer agrees with my digestion, I fear, but I can offer you a cup of iced milk, sweetened with honey. I find it most refreshing in this heat." —A GAME OF THRONES

Serves 1 ✦ Prep: 5 minutes ✦ Chilling: 1 hour at least

*Pairs well with Modern Honey Biscuits (page 115),
Modern Cheese-and-Onion Pie (page 145)*

For many of us, pouring milk over ice is counterintuitive, but the addition of the honey makes this more than milk. It's clean and refreshing, and if you use the spices, you'll find they lend it a subtle, exotic feel. Definitely a must for the hot, muggy weather of summer in King's Landing.

1 cup part-skim or whole milk	Pinch of saffron and/or cinnamon
2 tablespoons honey, or to taste	(optional)

Pour milk into a saucepan and warm it over low heat. Do not scald the milk! When steam begins to rise from the surface, add the honey and stir until combined. Place the sweetened milk in the fridge to cool off.

To serve, place either cubes or small chunks of ice (crushed ice dissolves too quickly) into a glass. Pour the sweetened milk over the ice, sprinkle with spices, if desired, and serve.

Dorne

✦ ✦ ✦

Breakfast in Dorne

Flatbread ✦ Chickpea Paste

Stuffed Grape Leaves

Dornish Snake with Fiery Sauce

Duck with Lemons ✦ Lemonsweet

Breakfast in Dorne

[T]hey broke their fast on honeycakes baked with blackberries and nuts, gammon steaks, bacon, fingerfish crisped in breadcrumbs, autumn pears, and a Dornish dish of onions, cheese, and chopped eggs cooked up with fiery peppers. —A STORM OF SWORDS

Serves 3 to 4 ✦ Prep: 10 minutes ✦ Cooking: 25 minutes

Pairs well with Flatbread (page 175),
Fingerfish (page 120), Lemonsweet (page 187)

If you like spicy food, you will enjoy this breakfast. It is a warm scramble of eggs with onion, cheese, and pepper, served with a heap of sautéed onions and fiery peppers. The result is a mouthwatering medley of flavors that embodies the heat of the Dornish landscape and the fiery pride of the Dornish people. Although this dish is very spicy, the heat is not cumulative. It quickly becomes hot, but it maintains that same mouthwatering level of heat straight through to the end.

1 jalapeño pepper	4 or 5 tablespoons olive oil, plus
1 green cubanelle pepper	more if needed
1 orange bell pepper	1 ice cube
2 cherry bell peppers, in different	6 eggs
colors	¼ cup grated cheddar cheese
2 poblano peppers, red and green	3 pinches of salt
1 medium onion, coarsely chopped	Ground black pepper

Chop all the peppers roughly. Take a colorful mixture of these pepper pieces and mince enough to make about 3 tablespoons; set this aside. Likewise, mince 3 tablespoons of the onions and set aside.

Pour 4 or 5 tablespoons of olive oil into a pan over medium heat. Add the coarsely chopped onion and sauté for 3 to 4 minutes, until the pieces are just starting to soften. Add the coarsely chopped peppers, and additional oil as needed to keep the peppers from burning. Sauté for another 3 minutes over medium heat, stirring often. Reduce the heat to medium low, add the ice cube, cover the pan, and steam the vegetables for 5 to 7 minutes, or until the peppers are somewhat softened. Transfer the vegetables to a plate and keep them warm.

In the same pan, sauté the reserved minced onions and peppers over low heat for about 1 minute. Add the eggs, but do not stir. Sprinkle the cheese over the eggs as they begin to cook, then add the salt and about 1 teaspoon pepper. Then scramble the eggs, keeping them moving in the pan until the whites cease to be runny. The moment this occurs, immediately remove the pan from the heat.

Serve the eggs and peppers side by side. Grind a little more black pepper over the eggs for presentation.

+ *Cook's Note:* We've listed the peppers that we used to make this dish, but you should improvise according to your spice sensitivity. Still, we would insist on including at least one orange or yellow bell pepper. These are sweet rather than spicy, but will pick up some of the heat of the other peppers in the pan.

Flatbread

A serving man brought [Doran Martell] a bowl of purple olives, with flatbread, cheese, and chickpea paste. He ate a bit of it, and drank a cup of the sweet, heavy strongwine that he loved. —A FEAST FOR CROWS

Traditional Flatbread

Makes 4 flat loaves + Prep: 15 minutes
Rising: 2 hours total + Baking: 6 to 8 minutes

*Pairs well with Duck with Lemons (page 184),
Chickpea Paste (page 179), wildflower honey, sweet wine*

This is a traditional Turkish recipe and could easily grace a table in Dorne. It results in a wonderfully soft and addictive bread that is equally good with honey, hummus, or a meat course.

1½ cups water

4½ teaspoons dry yeast (2 packets)

1 teaspoon sugar

4 cups flour, plus more as needed

1 teaspoon salt

3 tablespoons olive oil

1 egg, beaten, for glaze

Black sesame or poppy seeds
   (optional)

To make the sponge, heat ½ cup of the water until it is just warm, then dissolve the yeast and sugar in the water and let the mixture stand in a warm place for 10 minutes, until frothy. Stir in ½ cup of the flour, cover the bowl loosely with plastic wrap, and let rise for 30 minutes.

Heat the remaining 1 cup water until it is lukewarm. Put the remaining 3½ cups flour in a large bowl, make a well in the center, and add the sponge, salt, olive oil, and lukewarm water. Gradually work this into the flour to make a soft, sticky dough.

Knead the dough on a floured surface for 15 minutes, then put the dough in a buttered bowl, cover loosely, and let rise for 1 hour.

Punch the dough down and divide it into quarters, shaping each into a ball. Then loosely cover the balls and let them rest for an additional 30 minutes.

Preheat the oven to 550°F.

Wet your hands and shape each piece of dough into a circle by flattening the dough and stretching it to about a ½-inch thickness. Glaze the round with a generous amount of egg and sprinkle it with seeds, if desired. Press your fingertips firmly into the dough, creating indentations over the whole surface. Bake for 6 to 8 minutes, or until golden. The bread is best served warm with honey, but will keep for several days in an airtight container.

Modern Flatbread

Makes 15 to 20 small flatbreads
Prep: 10 minutes ✦ Rising: 1 hour ✦ Baking: 3 to 5 minutes each

Pairs well with Chickpea Paste (page 179),
Modern Bean-and-Bacon Soup (page 33),
olives, feta cheese, honey, sweet wine

This is a straightforward recipe for pita bread and is easy to make. Each piece comes steaming hot from the oven, easy to split open and stuff with your choice of filling.

2¼ teaspoons dry yeast (1 packet)   3 cups all-purpose flour
1 teaspoon honey   1¼ teaspoons salt
1½ cups warm water

Dissolve the yeast in ½ cup of warm water. Add in the honey and stir until dissolved. Let the mixture sit for 10 or 15 minutes until the water is foamy.

Combine the flour and salt in large bowl. Make a small depression in the middle of flour and pour the yeast mixture into the depression.

Slowly add the remaining 1 cup of water, and stir with a wooden spoon or rubber spatula until the dough is elastic. Then place it on a floured surface and knead for 10 to 15 minutes. When the dough is no longer sticky but is smooth and bounces back after being poked, it has been successfully kneaded. Place the dough in a greased bowl. Turn the dough upside down so the surface is thoroughly coated. Cover and allow it to sit in a warm place for about 1 hour, or until it has doubled in size.

Punch the dough down and roll it out into a rope; pinch it into 10 to 12 equal-size pieces and form them into balls. Place them on a floured surface, then let them sit, covered, for 10 minutes.

Set the rack at the very bottom of the oven, place your pizza stone or baking sheet on it, and preheat the oven to 500°F.

Using a rolling pin, roll out each ball of dough into a round 5 or 6 inches across and ¼-inch thick. On a pizza stone or preheated baking sheet, bake each pita for just a few minutes, until the bread puffs up and slightly browns. Then turn it over and bake for another minute. Depending on the size of your baking surface, you can bake several pitas at once. Remove each pita with a spatula from the baking sheet and replace with additional disks of dough for baking. Use the spatula to gently press each of the baked pitas flat, taking care to avoid the escaping steam. Devour while still warm.

+ *Cook's Note:* Baked pita bread can be stored for up to 1 week in airtight bags, and up to 1 month in the freezer. Be sure to use freezer bags when storing in the freezer.

Chickpea Paste

Serves 4 to 6 + Prep: 10 minutes total

*Pairs well with Flatbread (page 175), mixed olives,
Stuffed Grape Leaves (page 180), Lemonsweet (page 187)*

Commonly know as hummus, this dish is a staple in the Arabic world, and has been
since ancient times. Equally good as a side with larger meals, this puree is perfect for
a light lunch, scooped up with bits of flatbread. It's so simple to make at home that
it could quickly become a favorite snack!

1 or 2 cloves garlic

One 19-ounce can garbanzo beans,
   with half the liquid reserved

¼ cup lemon juice

2 tablespoons tahini

1 teaspoon salt

2 tablespoons olive oil

Aleppo pepper, or paprika
   (optional)

In a food processor, chop the garlic, then add the garbanzo beans, reserving about
1 tablespoon whole beans for garnish. Add the lemon juice, tahini, and salt to the
mix. Blend until creamy and well mixed, adding reserved bean liquid as needed.

Transfer the mixture to a medium serving bowl. Make a decorative imprint in the
top, drizzle with olive oil, and sprinkle with Aleppo pepper to taste. Garnish with the
reserved garbanzo beans.

Stuffed Grape Leaves

The kid had been roasted with lemon and honey. With it were grape leaves stuffed with a mélange of raisins, onions, mushrooms, and fiery dragon peppers. "I am not hungry," Arianne said. . . . After a while, hunger weakened her resolve, so she sat and ate." —A FEAST FOR CROWS

Makes about 20 stuffed grape leaves
Prep: 45 minutes + Cooking: 40 minutes to 1 hour

Pairs well with olives, feta cheese, dates, dry red wine

We took a traditional Mediterranean recipe for stuffed grape leaves and added what was needed in order to make it properly Dornish, according to the description: raisins, mushrooms, lamb, and "fiery dragon peppers."

1 pint jar brined grape leaves, drained	7 to 10 crimini or button mushrooms, minced
1 medium onion, minced	¼ pound ground lamb
½ tablespoon extra-virgin olive oil	1 handful chopped raisins
1 teaspoon hot pepper, such as jalapeño, finely minced	1 cup cooked rice
¼ teaspoon ground black pepper	¼ cup chicken stock
½ teaspoon sea salt	Juice of ½ lemon

Carefully remove the leaves from the jar; they are tightly rolled and squeezed in and can rip when you are pulling them out. Unroll the leaves and gently peel them apart. Place them in a large bowl, cover them with boiling water, and soak for 30 minutes. Rinse with cold water to remove some of the brine. If they are very salty, you may wish to repeat the soaking and rinsing process.

In a skillet, over medium heat, sauté the onion in the oil until the pieces begin to caramelize. Add the hot pepper, black pepper, salt, and mushrooms. Cook for just a few minutes, until the mushrooms are soft. Remove the pan from the heat and add the raw ground lamb, raisins, and rice, mixing everything together in a bowl. Don't cook this mixture but simply blend it well.

Choose a grape leaf to fill—the best ones are about the size of your palm—and lay it on a work surface, vein side up. Place about 1½ tablespoons of the meat mixture near the stem end, then fold in the end and sides and neatly roll up the packet. Repeat this process until all of the filling is gone.

Line the bottom of a large, heavy-bottomed pot with several unstuffed grape leaves, then arrange as many filled rolls as will fit in a snug layer on top, seam sides down. Put down more unstuffed leaves, then place a second layer of rolls on top, positioning them perpendicular to those in the previous layer. When all the rolls are in the pot, pour in the stock, then drizzle the lemon juice over the grape leaves. If there are any leaves left over, place them on top of the rolls. Set a heatproof dish directly on top of the rolls to keep them pressed down.

Cover the pot with a lid and simmer slowly over medium-low heat for 45 minutes to 1 hour, or until the leaves are tender, the meat is cooked, and the filling is soft; take one of the rolls out of the pot to test it for doneness. You may need to add more liquid during cooking. If so, add ½ cup water and continue to simmer for another 15 minutes. When the rolls are done, let them cool. Serve them at room temperature.

+ *Cook's Note:* You can make these rolls up to 3 days in advance, then remove them from the fridge 1 or 2 hours before you need them. You can also reheat them in a microwave.

Dornish Snake with Fiery Sauce

A short man stood in an arched doorway, grilling chunks of snake over a brazier, turning them with wooden tongs as they crisped. The pungent smell of his sauces brought tears to the knight's eyes. The best snake sauce had a drop of venom in it, he had heard, along with mustard seeds and dragon peppers. —A FEAST FOR CROWS

Serves 4 as a light meal ✦ Prep: 5 minutes
Grilling: 15 to 20 minutes ✦ Sauce: 15 minutes

Pairs well with olives, feta cheese, Flatbread (page 175), sweet red wine

While many claim that snake tastes just like chicken, this is not strictly the case. The texture is similar to chicken—but a slightly overcooked one, quite firm. It's reminiscent of a dried sausage, given the leanness of the meat and its density. The flavor, admittedly, does share some similarities with chicken, but this is only insofar as both chicken and snake are relatively mild, as if designed to showcase whatever they are served with. In this case, the sauce steals the spotlight. Warm, rich, with a bit of a bite to it, the sauce is subtly exotic. However, it is not so strong that it overpowers the flavor of the snake and instead complements the slight gaminess of the meat.

1 rattlesnake, approximately
   2 pounds, cleaned and gutted
Unsalted butter
4 tablespoons stone-ground
   mustard
2 teaspoons spicy peppers
   such as ancho, according to
   your comfort level

⅔ cup red wine
2 tablespoons olive oil
2 teaspoons lemon juice
2 tablespoons honey
1 teaspoon turmeric

Heat a grill to medium high.

Coil the snake and place it on a piece of tinfoil. Slice off a few pats of butter and place them on or around the snake. Wrap the snake in a couple layers of foil. Place it on the hot grill and cook it for 15 minutes. Then unwrap it and cook it directly on the grill for 2 minutes on each side. Remove it to a decorative plate and keep it warm.

In a small saucepan, combine the mustard, peppers, wine, oil, lemon juice, honey, and turmeric. Keep the sauce on a low simmer until it has reduced by at least a third, about 15 minutes. Pour it into a decorative dish and serve it alongside the snake for dipping.

Duck with Lemons

Anguy shuffled his feet. "We were thinking we might eat it, Sharna. With lemons. If you had some."

"Lemons. And where would we get lemons? Does this look like Dorne to you, you freckled fool? Why don't you hop out back to the lemon trees and pick us a bushel, and some nice olives and pomegranates too."

—A STORM OF SWORDS

Serves 3 to 4 ✦ Prep: 15 minutes
Sauce: 10 minutes ✦ Cooking: 2 hours

Pairs well with Traditional Flatbread (page 175),
Medieval Honey Biscuits (page 114), Lemonsweet (page 187)

The glaze on this duck is amazing, and the sweet tang of lemons bursts onto the tongue like a Sand Snake out of an ambush. Then comes the clash as lemon, gamey duck, and fiery peppers war with one another. The spice wins out in the end, the slow burn spreading to the back of the throat. It verges on overpowering, but then fades pleasantly, leaving you longing for the next bite.

2 lemons

1 duck, about 4 pounds

½ cup lemon juice (1 to 2 lemons)

3 tablespoons olive oil, plus more
    for the duck

½ teaspoon table salt

2 tablespoons honey

1 teaspoon ground chili powder

¼ teaspoon white pepper

Kosher salt

2 pounds assorted root vegetables
    such as potatoes, carrots, and
    leeks, cut into chunks (optional)

Preheat the oven to 375°F.

Juice your lemons and stuff the empty lemon halves into the duck. Pour ½ cup of

the lemon juice into a small saucepan over medium heat and reserve any remaining lemon juice for another purpose. Add the oil, table salt, honey, and spices to the pan. Simmer this sauce until it has just begun to reduce, about 5 minutes.

Place the duck in a roasting pan. Truss the legs and fold the wing tips in so they don't burn. Rub the duck down with olive oil, then sprinkle it with kosher salt. Using a basting brush, apply the glaze to both sides of the duck.

If you like, add your choice of vegetables to the pan; they will cook in the duck fat.

Roast the duck for 1 hour. Take it out of the oven to baste with additional glaze, then continue cooking for 45 minutes longer. Apply more glaze, then cook for 15 more minutes, or until golden brown. Give the bird one last treatment of glaze, and serve with the vegetables on the side, if you wish.

+ *Cook's Note:* After you've eaten the meat from the duck, boil down the carcass for a few hours to make broth. It is absolutely wonderful when used to make risotto.

Lemonsweet

Arianne drew the child away. "You must be hungry. We have dates and cheese and olives, and lemonsweet to drink. You ought not eat or drink too much, though." —A FEAST FOR CROWS

17th-Century Lemonsweet

Serves 6 to 8 + Prep: 10 minutes

Pairs well with Flatbread (page 175) and Chickpea Paste (page 179), Stuffed Grape Leaves (page 180), dried fruit, blood oranges

This is an intense, flavorful version of lemonade, with all the vibrancy of fresh citrus and a sweet tang that goes on and on. It also tastes great with a touch of nontraditional carbonation.

Limonade. Prenez une pinte d'eau, mettez de-dans demie livre de sucre, le jus de six citrons & de deaux oranges, l'écorce de la moitié d'un citron & d'une orange que vousaurez pressé. Battez bien l'eau dans deux vaisseaux bien nets en la versand l'un dans l'autre plusieurs fois, & la passez une serviette blanche.
—LE CONFITURIER FRANÇAIS, 17TH CENTURY

6 lemons	2¼ cups confectioners' sugar
2 oranges	2½ cups still or sparkling water

Zest half a lemon and half an orange.

Juice the lemons and oranges into a large pitcher or bowl. Add the sugar and peel, then stir or shake vigorously. Pour the lemonade through a cloth or paper towel to strain out the zest and citrus pips. Add water and serve chilled. Keep refrigerated.

Modern Lemonsweet with Honey and Vanilla

Serves 4 ✦ Prep: 10 minutes

Pairs well with Flatbread (page 175) and Chickpea Paste (page 179),
Modern Grilled Peaches in Honey (page 160), olives

This modern recipe, ironically, makes lemonade that tastes very old-world. Using honey instead of sugar reduces the immediate sweetness prevalent in many modern lemonades, while the unexpected taste of the vanilla will make you stop and work the flavors over again in your mouth.

½ cup honey

2 cups water

1 vanilla bean, or

    ½ teaspoon vanilla

    extract

1 sprig fresh thyme or

    rosemary (optional)

6 or 7 lemons

Lemon wheels or wedges,

    for garnish

In a large saucepan over medium-high heat, combine the honey and 2 cups water. Slit the vanilla bean in half lengthwise, then, using the back of the knife, scrape the seeds out of the pod and into the saucepan, then drop the pod in as well. Bring the mixture to a boil and cook for 4 or 5 minutes, until the honey is dissolved and the mixture thickens. Remove it from the heat, add your herb sprig if desired, and allow to cool.

Squeeze enough of the lemons to make 1½ cups juice and pour it into a gallon jug or pitcher. Cut a whole lemon into wheels or wedges and set them aside to use as garnish.

Pour the honey syrup through a strainer into the pitcher. Add water to equal 1 gallon and stir well. Serve the lemonade over ice, garnished with lemon wheels or wedges.

Across the Narrow Sea

✦ ✦ ✦

Breakfast in Meereen

Biscuits and Bacon ✦ Honey-Spiced Locusts

Beet Soup ✦ Tyroshi Honeyfingers

Wintercakes ✦ Tyroshi Pear Brandy

Iced Green Minty Drink

Honey-Sweetened Wine

Breakfast in Meereen

Dany broke her fast under the persimmon tree that grew in the terrace garden. . . . Missandei served her duck eggs and dog sausage, and half a cup of sweetened wine mixed with the juice of a lime. The honey drew flies, but a scented candle drove them off. —A STORM OF SWORDS

Serves 2 ✦ Eggs: Several hours to overnight
Prep: 10 minutes ✦ Cooking: 30 minutes

Pairs well with Honey-Sweetened Wine (page 216)

This is one of the more decadent breakfasts to be found in Westeros or Essos. Tea eggs are a wonderfully simple way to make hard-boiled eggs interesting and exciting. The yolks stay creamy even after they are cooked; this, combined with the subtle flavors imparted by its tea, is a spicy and exotic variation on the common egg. We recommend pairing them with a lamb sausage, a suitably unusual breakfast meat. Consider serving the Honey-Sweetened Wine as well; it is an exquisite addition to the meal, complementing the sweetness of the fresh fruit and balancing the richness of meat and eggs.

4 hard-boiled eggs, preferably duck
    eggs (see page 15)

3 black tea bags

1 teaspoon ground cinnamon

½ teaspoon ground clove

1 star anise

½ cup soy sauce

4 sausages, your favorite kind

Persimmon, figs, dates, or other
    fruit (optional)

Using the back of a spoon, gently crack the shells of the hard-boiled eggs all the way around so there are spiderweb-like lines all over the shells. Place them back in the pot and cover them with water. To the pot, add the tea bags, spices, and soy sauce. Simmer the eggs in this mixture for 30 minutes, then either continue to simmer for another few hours, or soak them overnight. At this point, you can either chill the eggs for up to a week and serve them cold, or you can serve them warm.

When you're ready to serve, peel the eggs, taking care to just remove the shell and the outer membrane and to preserve the beautiful cracked pattern on the egg white.

Cook the sausages according to your preference, slice up some fruit, arrange everything on the plates, and serve.

+ *Cook's Note:* Both the eggs (and the wine, if you choose to serve it) require time to steep, and are best prepared the day before.

Biscuits and Bacon

Ysilla was turning the biscuits. She laid an iron pan atop the brazier and put the bacon in. Some days she cooked biscuits and bacon; some days bacon and biscuits. Once every fortnight there might be a fish, but not today. . . . They were best when eaten hot, dripping with honey and butter. —A DANCE WITH DRAGONS

Serves 4 ♦ Prep: 10 minutes
Biscuits: 15 minutes ♦ Gravy: 10 minutes

Pairs well with Medieval Pease Porridge (page 38),
Modern Beet Pancakes (page 66),
Sister's Stew (page 90)

Like many of our modern recipe interpretations, this one is a bit loose. We doubt that Ysilla would have the means to make this particular pairing on the deck of a ship, but it was too delicious to pass up.

2 cups plus 2 tablespoons
    all-purpose flour
1 tablespoon baking powder
Salt
3 cups milk (whatever is in
    the fridge)

2 teaspoons unsalted butter,
    melted
6 slices bacon
Ground black pepper

Preheat the oven to 450°F and grease a baking sheet.

In a bowl, combine 2 cups flour, the baking powder, and ¼ teaspoon salt. Combine 1 cup of the milk and the butter, then stir this into the dry ingredients until just blended. Drop the biscuits by rounded tablespoonfuls onto the baking sheet. Bake for 10 to 12 minutes, or until golden brown.

While the biscuits bake, preheat a large skillet over medium-high heat. Place the bacon in the skillet and cook until it is just shy of crispy. Set it aside to drain on paper towels. Discard all but 2 tablespoons of the bacon grease. Add the remaining 2 tablespoons of flour to the grease, and whisk it in thoroughly. Cook for about 1 minute, taking care not to burn the flour. Then add the remaining 2 cups milk and whisk thoroughly. Heat the mixture until bubbling, then simmer for 5 to 10 minutes, until it starts to thicken. Meanwhile, crumble the bacon and add it to the gravy along with generous amounts of salt and pepper. Allow the gravy to simmer until the desired consistency is achieved, then serve it over the biscuits.

Honey-Spiced Locusts

*Hizdahr had stocked their box with flagons of chilled wine and sweetwater,
with figs, dates, melons, and pomegranates, with pecans and peppers and
a big bowl of honeyed locusts. Strong Belwas bellowed, "Locusts!" as he
seized the bowl and began to crunch them by the handful.*

—A DANCE WITH DRAGONS

Makes 1 cup of cooked insects
Prep: 15 minutes ✦ Cooking: 10 minutes

Pairs well with exotic fruits, Honey-Sweetened Wine (page 216)

This Volantene recipe results in a sweet and spicy, super crunchy snack. It takes a bit
of psychological adjustment to get over the idea of eating bugs ... but the novelty
and brag factor make it well worth the effort. Underlying the more familiar tastes of
honey and spice is the real flavor of the crickets—a sort of smoky nuttiness that takes
several crickets' worth to savor.

4 tablespoons (½ stick)	Pinch of salt
unsalted butter	2 tablespoons honey
1 cup freeze-dried crickets	1 teaspoon Aleppo pepper
or locusts	or paprika

Preheat the oven to 200°F.

Melt the butter in a pan over medium heat. Add the insects and salt and stir gently for around 10 minutes, making sure to completely coat them in butter.

In a small bowl, combine the honey and the Aleppo pepper. When the bugs are suitably crisped, drizzle the mixture over them and stir a bit more.

Spread the crickets on a baking sheet lined with parchment paper and bake for around 10 minutes, until the bugs are no longer quite so sticky. Serve immediately, or store in an airtight container for up to 2 days.

Beet Soup

Sweet beets were grown in profusion hereabouts, and were served with almost every meal. The Volantenes made a cold soup of them, as thick and rich as purple honey. —A DANCE WITH DRAGONS

Roman-style Beet Soup

Serves 4 ✦ Prep: 10 minutes ✦ Cooking: 45 minutes to 1 hour

*Pairs well with Black Bread (page 85),
Roman Buttered Carrots (page 137), red wine*

This Roman recipe is the less familiar of the two beet soups in this book, and more rustic than your average borscht. The vegetables, especially the leeks, don't quite break down when mashed, which gives the soup a hearty texture with an earthy taste.

Concides porrum, coriandrum, cuminum, uuam passam, farinam et omnia in medullam mittes. ligabis et ita inferes ex liquamine, oleo et aceto.

—APICIUS, 1ST CENTURY

Olive oil

2 leeks (white and light green parts only), well washed and cut into ½-inch slices

½ teaspoon ground coriander

½ teaspoon ground cumin

¾ cup wine (red or white, whatever you're drinking)

1 cup beef or chicken broth or water

⅓ cup red wine vinegar

4 medium beets, peeled and finely diced

Drizzle some olive oil into a medium saucepan. Add the leeks and the spices and cook, stirring gently to keep them from burning. When the leeks are golden, after about 5 minutes, add the wine, broth, vinegar, and beets. Cover and simmer until the beets are fork-tender, 45 minutes to 1 hour. Drain off the liquid and reserve it, then mash the beets and leeks in the pot, adding the reserved broth as needed. Ladle into individual bowls and serve hot or cold.

Modern Beet Soup

Serves 4 to 6 + Prep: 5 minutes + Cooking: about 40 minutes

Pairs well with Crusty White Bread (page 25),
Fish Tarts (page 140), meat pies, red wine

This soup is simple, wholesome, and hearty, with a lovely smooth texture that borscht is known for. It showcases all the best aspects of root vegetables. For a seasonal change, make it with water in the spring and summer and with beef stock in the fall and winter. The beef gives it a little more heartiness that will warm you to the core in cold months, while the warm-weather version can be served hot or cold, like a gazpacho.

1 medium yellow onion	2 potatoes
1 medium carrot	1 pound beets
1 clove garlic	Unsalted butter
4 cups water or beef broth	

Roughly chop all the vegetables, but keep them separate.

In a medium saucepan over medium heat, melt enough butter to coat the bottom of the pan, then add the onion, carrot, garlic, and a splash of the water or broth, and cover. Cook until the vegetables are soft and the onion is glossy. Add the potatoes, beets, and remaining water or broth, and simmer, mostly covered, until you can slide a fork in and out of the potatoes and beets without any resistance, about 30 minutes. Remove the soup from the heat and puree it, either with an immersion blender, or in small batches with a standard blender.

Finished soup may be served hot or chilled.

Tyroshi Honeyfingers

"[W]e seldom had enough coin to buy anything . . . well, except for a sausage now and again, or honeyfingers . . . do they have honeyfingers in the Seven Kingdoms, the kind they bake in Tyrosh?" —A GAME OF THRONES

Roman Honeyfingers

Makes 30 to 40 honeyfingers
Prep: 15 minutes + Cooking: 20 minutes

Pairs well with Beet Soup (page 199),
Rack of Lamb (page 42), Iced Milk with Honey (page 169)

This recipe is a curiosity. The honeyfingers fry to a crispy crunch on the outside while remaining a bit chewy on the inside. The pieces are easy to cut into shapes, and could probably even be rolled into logs. The flavor is really all about the honey, but the pepper and cinnamon on top, as well as the pine nuts, add a slight complexity.

piper, nucleos, mel, rutam et passum teres, cum lacte et tracta coques. coagulum coque cum modicis ovis . . . ita ut durissimam pultem facias, deinde in patellam expandis. cum refrixerit, concidis quasi dulcia et frigis in oleo optimo. levas, perfundis mel, piper aspargis et inferes. melius feceris, si lac pro aqua miseris.

—APICIUS, 4TH CENTURY

⅔ cup plus ¾ cup flour

1 cup whole milk (goat or cow)

Olive oil

2 tablespoons cooking sherry or
   sweet wine

1 egg, beaten

⅓ cup pine nuts, finely chopped

Cinnamon to taste

Ground black pepper to taste

1 cup honey, or more if needed

Chopped pine nuts for garnish

In a medium saucepan, whisk the ⅔ cup flour a little at a time into the cold milk so that there are no lumps. Add 1 tablespoon of the oil and the sherry, and cook on medium-high heat, stirring constantly, until a thick porridge forms. Remove the pan from the heat and continue to stir briskly to cool the mixture.

When the porridge is lukewarm, add the egg and stir briskly until it is blended. Stir in the pine nuts and a dash of cinnamon and pepper. Stir in the remaining ¾ cup flour to make a dough that is sticky but can still be handled.

On a floured board with floured hands, press the dough out to a ½-inch-thick rectangle; cut it into finger-size strips.

Cover the bottom of a frying pan with a layer of olive oil about ½ inch deep. Heat the oil and fry the strips of dough until they are golden brown and crispy. Remove the fried strips to a plate covered with paper towels to drain. Dip them in honey and sprinkle them with cinnamon and pine nuts.

Modern Honeyfingers

Makes 15 to 18 honeyfingers ✦ Syrup: 3 hours to overnight
Dough: 2 hours ✦ Frying: 20 minutes

Pairs well with Sweet Pumpkin Soup (page 131),
Quails Drowned in Butter (page 154), Iced Milk with Honey (page 169)

Delighted with the spiced sauce and the incredibly luscious texture, you will find yourself gobbling up these pastries and shamelessly licking your fingers. The braided fritters are impressive in presentation, yet reminiscent of fried dough from country fairs.

For the Syrup:

1 cup sugar

1 cup water

1 cup honey

1 tablespoon fresh ginger, grated

Pinch of salt

1 tablespoon lemon juice

1 stick cinnamon

For the Dough:

2 cups cake flour

2½ teaspoons baking powder

½ teaspoon salt

2 tablespoons unsalted butter,
chilled and cut into pieces

¼ cup whole milk

¼ cup water

1 teaspoon lemon juice

Oil for frying

Cook all the ingredients for the syrup in a pan over medium heat, stirring until the sugar dissolves. Bring the syrup to a boil, then cover it with the lid and allow it to boil for 1 minute.

Uncover the pan, then turn down the heat to medium high and let the syrup simmer for about 5 minutes. Chill the syrup in the fridge for several hours, or overnight. It should be ice cold when you make the honeyfingers.

To make the dough, combine the flour, baking powder, and salt in a large bowl. Rub in the butter until the mixture resembles bread crumbs.

Make a well in the middle of the bowl and pour in the remaining ingredients, except for the oil. Mix thoroughly, then turn the dough out onto a floured surface and knead for about 5 minutes until it is soft and elastic, but not sticky. It should be of a consistency that it can be rolled out easily. Cover the dough with plastic wrap and allow it to rest for 2 hours.

Roll the dough out to a ¼-inch-thick rectangle, then cut it into strips about ½-inch wide. You can decide your desired length. Braid 3 strips of the same length together, pinching the ends well to prevent them from unraveling. Do this with all the dough. The braids should be 6 to 8 inches long.

Place the chilled syrup in a larger bowl of ice water to help keep it cold and set it near your stove. Heat about 1 inch oil over medium heat until it is very hot. Carefully drop the braided fingers a couple at a time into the oil and fry them for just a few minutes until they're golden on both sides. Remove the honeyfingers from the oil and plunge them into the cold syrup. Leave them in the syrup until they have stopped cooking, about 30 seconds.

Pull the finished honeyfingers from the syrup mixture and set on a cooling rack with parchment paper or a cookie sheet underneath to catch the dripping syrup. Serve immediately once all the honeyfingers have been fried and cooled in syrup.

Wintercakes

He could still recall the sounds of the three bells, the way that Noom's deep peals set his very bones to shuddering, the proud strong voice of Narrah, sweet Nyel's silvery laughter. The taste of wintercake filled his mouth again, rich with ginger and pine nuts and bits of cherry . . .

—A FEAST FOR CROWS

These Elizabethan cakes are dense and heavy, yet addictive. The overall taste is one of pleasant, homey shortbread, but when you get a bite with cherry or ginger, the flavor shifts from familiar to foreign and fantastic. Consider eating them with your afternoon tea or coffee while lounging in a large armchair.

Elizabethan Wintercakes

Makes 12 to 14 cakes

Prep: 15 minutes ✦ Baking: 25 minutes

Pairs well with Cold Fruit Soup (page 59), Mulled Wine (page 48) or tea

We added dried cherries, pine nuts, and ginger to comply with our chosen historical recipe, but we decided to omit the icing. We found that it wasn't really needed when all was said and baked—but you are more than welcome to give it a go!

> *Take three pound and a half of very fine flower well dryed by the fire, and put to it a pound and half of loaf Sugar sifted in a very fine sieve and dryed; Three pounds of Currants well washed and dryed in a cloth and set by the fire; When your flower is well mixed with the Sugar and Currants, you must put in it a pound and half of unmelted butter, ten spoonfuls of Cream, with the yolks of three new-laid Eggs beat with it, one Nutmeg; and if you please, three spoonfuls of Sack. When you have wrought your paste well, you must put it in a cloth, and set it in a dish before the fire, till it be through warm. Then make them up in little Cakes, and prick them full of holes; you must bake them in a quick oven unclosed. Afterwards Ice them over with Sugar.*
>
> —THE CLOSET OF SIR KENELM DIGBY KNIGHT OPENED, 1669

3½ cups all-purpose flour

¾ cup sugar

1 cup (2 sticks) unsalted butter, softened

½ cup dried cherries, diced

¼ cup candied ginger, diced

⅓ cup pine nuts

5 tablespoons double cream (or heavy cream)

2 egg yolks

1 teaspoon grated nutmeg

2 tablespoons sweet white wine, such as marsala or sherry, plus more if needed

Preheat the oven to 375°F and grease a baking sheet.

Combine the flour and sugar in a bowl. Rub in the butter, then add the dried cherries, ginger, and pine nuts. In a separate bowl, mix the cream and egg yolks, then pour this over the dry mixture. Stir in the nutmeg and wine, combining everything thoroughly until the dough holds together and forms one big ball (add a little more wine if needed).

Form the dough into disks about 4 inches across and ¾ inch thick and place them on the baking sheet, giving each cake room to spread a little. Bake the cakes for about 25 minutes, or until they are slightly golden on top.

Modern Wintercake

Serves 10 to 12

Prep: 30 minutes + Baking: 30 to 40 minutes

Pairs well with Modern Stewed Rabbit (page 96), cold apple cider

In the modern cake, the spice of the ginger combined with the tang of the cherries is reminiscent of an English fruitcake, but the texture is more like the interior of a moist, high-quality scone. It is incredibly flavorful and comforting—the perfect baked good to consume by a fire on a brisk winter day.

For the Cake:

¾ cup firmly packed brown sugar

⅓ cup unsalted butter, softened

½ cup sour cream

2 eggs

1 teaspoon vanilla

1½ cups all-purpose flour

1 teaspoon baking powder

½ teaspoon salt

½ teaspoon ground ginger

½ cup dried cherries, coarsely
    chopped

3 tablespoons candied ginger, diced

¼ cup pine nuts

For the Topping:

¼ cup firmly packed brown sugar

3 tablespoons unsalted butter,
    chilled

2 tablespoons candied ginger, diced

1 tablespoon flour

½ cup confectioners' sugar

1 to 2 teaspoons milk or cream

Preheat the oven to 350°F. Grease and flour a large angel-food cake pan.

In a large bowl, using a hand mixer (or in the bowl of a standing mixer), beat the brown sugar and butter together at medium speed, scraping the bowl often, until completely combined. Add the sour cream, eggs, and vanilla, and continue beating until well mixed. Reduce the speed to low and gradually add the flour, baking powder, salt, and ginger. Beat well. Using a wooden spoon, stir in the cherries, candied ginger, and pine nuts. Pour the batter into the baking pan and smooth it out.

In a separate bowl, mix together the brown sugar, cold butter, diced ginger, and flour. The mixture should be crumbly, and a food processor can help with this immensely. Sprinkle the mixture evenly over the top of the cake and bake it for 30 to 35 minutes, or until a toothpick inserted in the center comes out clean and the topping is golden brown. Let the cake cool for a short time in the pan, then transfer it to a rack.

In a small bowl, combine the confectioners' sugar and enough milk or cream to achieve the desired glazing consistency. Drizzle the glaze over the cooled cake, and serve.

Tyroshi Pear Brandy

"I have sweet reds, from Lys and Volantis and the Arbor, Whites from Lys, Tyroshi pear brandy, firewine, pepperwine . . ." —A GAME OF THRONES

Makes about 1 quart ✦ Prep: 20 minutes
Stewing: 1 month ✦ Aging: 1 to 3 months

*Pairs well with Roman Buttered Carrots (page 137),
Duck with Lemons (page 184), Modern Poached Pears (page 109)*

There is something innately satisfying about making this pear brandy. There's a fine feeling of anticipation as it ages in a dark corner of the house, its color slowly deepening. The brandy also improves considerably during this time. After the first month, it is harsh and unpleasant. At month two, it has obviously mellowed, and after the third month, it is wonderfully drinkable, full of all the best flavors of both brandy and pears.

1 cup sugar

1 cup water

1½ pounds ripe pears (3 to 4)

1 bottle brandy (750 ml.)

1 teaspoon fruit protector powder (optional)

Make a simple syrup by cooking the sugar and water over medium-high heat until the solution is clear. Allow the syrup to cool to room temperature.

Cut the pears into quarters, core them, and slice them thinly. Combine the pears, sugar syrup, brandy, and fruit protector (if using), in a clean 2-quart jar with a lid. Cover the jar and place it in a cool, dark place for 1 month. Don't refrigerate!

After a month, filter the liquid through cheesecloth into a new, clean container, removing the solids. Either discard the pear slices, or use them in another recipe. Allow the brandy to age for 1 to 3 months before serving. Store sealed for several years, or up to 1 year after initially opening.

✦ *Cook's Note:* Fruit protector powder is often used in home canning, and is made by well-known companies, such as Ball, Bernardin, and Mrs. Wages.

Iced Green Minty Drink

Slave girls scurried through light and shadow, bearing flagons of ale and wine and some iced green drink that smelled of mint. One table in twenty was occupied at this hour of the morning. —A DANCE WITH DRAGONS

Traditional Iced Green Minty Drink

Serves 4 + Prep: 5 minutes
Chilling: 2 hours to overnight

*Pairs well with Breakfast in Meereen (page 193),
Oatcakes (page 55), Fingerfish (page 120)*

This unique and flavorful beverage is traditional green tea, jazzed up. The sweetness and refreshing mint are well suited to hot days and climates, or for when you just need a nice crisp pick-me-up.

½ tablespoon loose matcha
green tea

4 cups boiling water

¼ cup honey, or to taste

1 cup fresh mint leaves,
loosely packed

4 small stalks lemongrass
for garnish

Pour the loose tea and boiling water into a 1- to 1½-quart teapot and steep the tea for 2 minutes. Stir in honey to taste, followed by the mint leaves, and steep for 3 to 4 minutes longer. At this point, you can either serve the tea hot in small heatproof glasses or chill it for a few hours. Serve it garnished with a stalk of lemongrass.

+ *Cook's Note:* This recipe is inspired by traditional Moroccan mint tea, but we've tweaked it a bit to make it more green, using powdered matcha green tea for color. Matcha green tea, a finely ground loose-leaf tea, has been used in the ancient Japanese tea ceremony since it was brought to Japan in 1191 by a Chinese Zen Buddhist monk.

Modern Iced Green Minty Drink

Serves 3 to 4 ✦ Prep: 5 minutes
Chilling: 2 hours to overnight

Pairs well with Breakfast in Meereen (page 193),
Duck with Lemons (page 184)

Light, cold, and refreshing, this beverage is tasty enough to be craved, and just exotic enough to suit the far reaches of Volantis. When first mixed, the icy slush is a uniform pale foamy concoction. After a few moments, however, it settles into three layers: the crushed ice is on top, pushing down on the melon puree, and the straight juice falls to the bottom. The mint flavor complements the melon, and just a bit of carbonation makes things interesting.

2 cups 1-inch cubed honeydew
    melon

3 cups crushed ice

½ cup packed fresh mint leaves

One 12-ounce bottle ginger ale

⅓ cup honey

Add all ingredients to a blender. Pulse until the mixture becomes slushy. Pour into glasses and serve immediately.

+ *Cook's Note:* **For a nice adult twist on this drink, try adding a splash of your favorite alcohol. We recommend vodka or Midori, but the recipe is well suited to experiment.**

Honey-Sweetened Wine

Dany broke her fast under the persimmon tree that grew in the terrace garden. . . . Missandei served her duck eggs and dog sausage, and half a cup of sweetened wine mixed with the juice of a lime. The honey drew flies, but a scented candle drove them off. —A STORM OF SWORDS

Makes 3 servings + Prep: 5 minutes
Chilling: 2 hours to overnight

*Pairs well with Breakfast in Meereen (page 193),
Duck with Lemons (page 184)*

This beverage is a variation on ancient Roman mulsum, and is very refreshing and drinkable on a warm summer morning.

12 ounces semisweet wine, white
or rosé

About 2 tablespoons honey
3 lime wedges

In a glass or pitcher, mix the wine and honey. The ratio is roughly 1 tablespoon honey per glass of wine, but add the honey slowly and sweeten to your taste. Squeeze the juice from one or two of the lime wedges into the mixture, and stir until everything has been incorporated. This beverage can be made ahead of time and chilled. To serve, pour it into three decorative glasses and garnish with the lime.

Feasting in Style

Cooking, eating, and drinking are closely tied to the Proustian memory, the experiences etched into our minds forever. When planning a feast, one must consider not only the food, but also the overall atmosphere. Serving dishes, lighting, flatware, table decor, beverages, and overall mood affect how your family and guests will experience a meal. You may have cooked your authentic Westerosi meal on your beautiful new gas range in your relatively high-tech kitchen, but when guests are seated and the meal is served, you can transport everyone to the decadence of King's Landing, the insulated comfort of Winterfell's halls, or the opulence of a magister's villa in Pentos.

Strive to make the table as much a tactile experience as the meal itself. Heavy rough-spun linen and furs reflect life in the North, while sheer silks and gilding are more suited to King's Landing. Choosing a tablecloth is the simplest way to begin the transformation—red for a Lannister meal, gray for a Stark, ornately woven fabrics from across the narrow sea, or a rough-spun black for meals with the Night's Watch. Likewise, props—antlers, silver bowls, autumn leaves, pine boughs, exotic fruits, and flowers—add something special to the meal. And don't skimp on the candles. Beautiful as well as authentic, candlelight creates a special experience.

Serving dishes and place settings should, ideally, reflect the location in which the guests mentally dine. Avoid starkly modern items, choosing instead earthenware casseroles, turned wooden bowls, and hammered flatware. Rather than the glasses given to you on your wedding day, opt for hefty pewter tankards and thick, handblown glass. Historical accuracy is not as important as creating an atmosphere consistent with the aesthetic of Ice and Fire. As modern consumers, we are so used to certain conveniences that something as simple as the absence of separate water and wineglasses will immediately distance the meal from an everyday culinary experience.

Thrift stores are a great way to inexpensively outfit a Westerosi table; they offer props, dishware, centerpieces, and cutlery. Also take a look through dusty attics and deep kitchen cabinets for items you may have forgotten.

Index

Menus

Dinner in King's Landing
Crusty White Bread, Summer Greens Salad, Buttered Carrots, White Beans and Bacon, Roasted Boar

Dinner with the Night's Watch
Rack of Lamb, Turnips in Butter, Salad at Castle Black, Iced Blueberries with Sweet Cream

Dinner at Riverrun
Trout Wrapped in Bacon, Summer Greens Salad, Pease Porridge, Crusty White Bread

A Feast at Winterfell
Aurochs Roasted with Leeks, Roasted Boar, Cold Fruit Soup, Oatcakes, Turnips in Butter, Baked Apples, Blueberry Tarts,

Poached Pears, wheels of white cheese, Mulled Wine, chilled autumn ale

Tourney Feast at King's Landing
Aurochs Roasted with Leeks, Crusty White Bread, Sansa Salad, Pigeon Pie, Baked Apples, Modern Lemon Cakes

Sumptuous Spread at Bitterbridge
Poached Pears, Fingerfish, Black Bread, Medieval Turnips in Butter, Cream Swans, Lemon Cakes, Honey Biscuits

A Wedding in King's Landing
Cream of Mushroom and Snail Soup, Pork Pie, Sweetcorn Fritters, Oatbread, Almond Crusted Trout, Cheese-and-Onion Pie, Fish Tarts, Pigeon Pie, Mulled Wine

Acknowledgments

First and foremost, we would like to thank George R. R. Martin, without whose work this cookbook obviously could not have been imagined. His world became ours years ago through his novels, and led us to explore the wonders of historical cookery. Only in our wildest dreams did we imagine that our culinary adventure would turn into this cookbook, so thank you for everything. The world needs its share of eaters, and we'll cook anything you like so long as you don't kill off too many main characters. . . .

We would like to thank a great number of others:

Our good friends, who put up with our monopolization of the kitchen for months on end, were patient while we photographed their cooling dinners, and without whose appetites we would have surely drowned in the sheer volume of food we cooked.

Percival, prince among cats, who made sure to taste everything that came out of the kitchen for quality assurance.

Our parents, not only for their continued faith in us, but also for their borrowed dishes, silverware, taxidermy, and backyards in which to build hazardous wildling fires.

Our fearless field agents, who delivered baskets of delicious goodies to George R. R. Martin during his book signing tour, braving crowds, public transportation, and pits of deadly vipers for the cause.

The terrific staff at Random House, for their belief in this project and invaluable help throughout the entire publishing process.

The loyal fans of our blog, whose enthusiasm and delight have kept us eager to try new Westerosi dishes long past what we would have been able to sustain by ourselves.

We would also like to thank the Vikings for mead, the Mesopotamians for beer, and that crazy Celt way back when who ate some spoiled apples, saw amazing things, and decided to make cider. . . .

About the Authors

Chelsea and Sariann co-run Inn at the Crossroads, a popular food blog based on the Song of Ice and Fire series. Both avid fans of the fantasy genre, they bring to the table a unique combination of artistry, historical knowledge, and love of food.

Chelsea grew up in rural New York, surrounded by cows and an appreciation for small farms. However, her real love affair with food began during a year abroad in Turkey, which sparked a passion for both food and history, as well as leading her to a degree in classical history. A lifelong artist and fantasy fan, she greatly enjoys foreign languages, treasure hunting, and all things honey.

Sariann learned her way around the kitchen at the sides of her mother and grandmothers. After growing up on a working New England farm, she attended the University of Vermont, where she spent time working on a dairy farm and became a supporter of the eating local and small farming movements. Something of a British cultural history enthusiast, she finds great pleasure in reinventing traditional staple dishes and rekindling love for foods that have been forgotten.

www.innatthecrossroads.com